DEATH

in Reverse

A Love Story

Ruth L. Schwartz

Michigan State University Press
East Lansing, Michigan

g green press INITIATIVE Michigan State University Press is a member of the Green Press Initiative and is committed to developing and encouraging ecologically responsible publishing practices. For more information about the Green Press Initiative and the use of recycled paper in book publishing, please visit www.greenpressinitiative.

∞ The paper used in this publication meets the minimum requirements of ANSI/NISO Z39.48-1992 (R 1997) (Permanence of Paper).

Michigan State University Press
East Lansing, Michigan 48823-5245

Printed and bound in the United States of America.

10 09 08 07 06 05 04   1 2 3 4 5 6 7 8 9 10

LIBRARY OF CONGRESS CATALOGING-IN-PUBLICATION DATA

Schwartz, Ruth L., 1962–
   Death in reverse : a love story / Ruth L. Schwartz.
      p.   cm.
   ISBN 0-87013-706-9
   1. Kidneys — Transplantation — Patients — United States — Biography.   2.
   Kidneys — Transplantation — Patients — Family relationships.   3.
   Kidneys — Transplantation — Complications.   4. Transplantation of organs,
   tissues, etc. — Anecdotes.   I. Title.
   RD575.S36 2004
   362.0197'4610592'0092 B 22

Cover design by Heather Truelove Aiston
Book design by Bookcomp, Inc.

Visit Michigan State University Press on the World Wide Web at:
   www.msupress.msu.edu

Author's Note

On May 11, 1995, I donated a kidney to my partner, Ana Rodriguez. This book documents the transplant, and the twelve months that followed.

This is a true story. However, the names of my partner and many other people in this book have been changed to protect their privacy.

This book is dedicated to the real Ana Rodriguez, to the past and present members of TRIO (Transplant Recipients International Organization), and to the many friends who helped us during this year, and beyond. We couldn't have done it without you!

I am particularly grateful to Alison, Julia, and Kyla, who were with me through some of the hardest times during those twelve months, and afterward. I am also deeply thankful for Anna Benassi's assistance–in the realms of both empathy and editing–as I readied the manuscript for publication. Héctor Carrillo provided invaluable help both by correcting my Spanish and by affirming that the story was worth telling. And I am indebted to Lillian Faderman for her ongoing support and encouragement–and to John Hales and the members of his Spring 2002 Creative Non-Fiction class at California State University, Fresno, for persuading me to seek publication at all.

Prologue

I'm at work when Ana calls to tell me our blood type matches.

"We're both A Positive. Isn't that wonderful?"

It *is* wonderful—and terrifying. There will be many months of tests to come before the doctors can tell me definitively that yes, I can be Ana's kidney donor. Yet, in this moment, I know.

I'd made the offer so casually. Years before, one of Ana's sisters had offered to give her a kidney when the time came. "And if your sister can't do it, I will," I'd told Ana blithely one day on the way to her nephrologist's office, confident that of course I wouldn't have to. That was the day Dr. Klinefeld explained to us that no one in Ana's family would be an eligible donor; her relatives all shared the same risk factors, the same genetic predisposition to kidney failure.

"What's your blood type?" he asked me. I didn't know. "Well, let's find out." And he called in a nurse who eased that first needle into the crook of my elbow, then filled a tube with my blood.

That was one of the days this story began.

Months later, I open my eyes to the blurred shapes of the hospital recovery room. Above me, a nurse fades in and out of view.

"Is the surgery over?" I ask, confused.

"Oh, yes. Everything went fine." And she disappears again, Cheshire cat–like.

Good, then. It's too late to back out. I'd been so afraid, through this last week, that I might lose my nerve.

▼

At this moment, a surgeon is suturing my right kidney and ureter into my lover's body.

⥥

Ana and I met in a 24-hour coffee shop on Market Street. She was wearing red, her favorite color, and sitting at a corner table, behind the revolving glass case filled with cakes and pies. She'd been eating a sandwich but stopped when she saw me watching her.

"You make me nervous," she said.

I apologized, not understanding at the time that the Spanish word *nerviosa* implies a pleasant kind of nervous tension, an anticipation.

"No, don't be sorry. It's been a long time since anyone has made me nervous." She looked at me intently, and I met her gaze. She was a handsome woman in her late thirties, big-boned and tall, with wavy black hair and piercing eyes.

"People have told me I look at them too hard," I admitted.

"That's funny. People have told me the same thing."

We talked a little about Puerto Rico, her homeland, and the upcoming elections there. I spoke Spanish to her, and she watched my mouth move.

"Would you like to come back to my apartment with me? It's quieter there. We can talk. I can make us some coffee," she suggested after a while.

And I almost didn't go. Her invitation seemed too forward to me. Still, something in my stomach moved. That something said *yes*.

"*What* was it that moved in your stomach?" my friend Alison has asked me many times since then. She's looking for her own true love, and wants to be sure not to miss him. Because of the transplant, because my kidney now works in Ana's body, cleansing her blood, the story of how we met and fell in love has been elevated to semi-mythological status.

Something moved in my stomach, I say. I'm not sure I've ever felt that exact sensation before or since. I followed the red taillights of Ana's car over the Market Street hill.

As she'd promised, she made us both instant coffee. We sat for a long time at her kitchen table. She told me about her brother Adrian, who lived with her and had AIDS. He was away on vacation that night. I told her I worked at the AIDS hotline, and suggested that she might want to volunteer. We must have talked of many other things as well, because the hours passed. It was past midnight and we hadn't touched.

"I feel so awkward in situations like this," I confessed. By this time we were seated together on her couch, side by side. Carefully, I set my coffee cup down on an end table. "I never know exactly what to do," I said.

"Just be yourself," Ana suggested. She sat perfectly still.

I put one hand on her shoulder then, on her gauzy red blouse. We were still on separate cliffs; there was a chasm between us. When I kissed her, I leaned over the cliff's edge.

<hr>

Today, many months after the transplant, I try to imagine my right kidney in the surgeon's palm. I know it would have been fist-sized, dark red, shaped roughly like the bean that bears its name. But did he hold it in both hands? And did it pulse as if breathing, the way one always imagines a heart?

In Western culture we've exalted the heart as the prime source of both life and love. In Chinese medicine, though, the kidneys are assigned even greater importance. They are astonishing organs, so critical to life that, as a safeguard, we are born with two—although we can live well with only one.

Inside each kidney is a vast network of tubules, connecting millions of tiny ports. These ports, which are called nephrons, work ceaselessly to filter our blood, distinguishing with infinite precision between those substances essential to our health and those that can poison us. Sometimes they are the same substance; with potassium, for instance, where minuscule amounts mean the difference between survival and death, it is the job of the kidneys to retain not a microgram more than the body needs.

When Ana and I were falling in love, she told me that she had been diabetic for over twenty years and that her kidneys would someday fail. Then, as new lovers often do, we ignored the threat, turning our attention to concerns that seemed more immediate. We had been together for four years when the crisis came.

Diabetes destroys the kidneys by strangling the nephrons, clogging them with toxins until they lose their ability to filter and excrete. During the final months of Ana's kidney failure I thought of her nephrons as a densely coiled, mile-long string of tiny white Christmas lights; as she grew weaker, as her skin turned gray, as her body began to ache from the poisons accumulating in her blood, I could see those lights winking out, sometimes one by one, other times a football-field's length at once—the way, when a single bulb goes, it may take with it all of the others on its string.

We'd known for years that Ana's kidneys were failing, and yet we didn't know. The kidneys are such "master chemists," as the books say, that people feel no symptoms of ill health until more than 80 percent of their kidney function is gone. Even then it is possible to feel quite well; it's not until function drops below 5 percent of normal that kidney failure becomes life-threatening.

At that point there are three ways to intervene. One is to undergo dialysis, a mechanical filtering process that crudely approximates the most critical of the kidney's functions. The second option (which many people do concurrently with the first) is to sign up on the kidney transplant waiting list, where most Americans wait an average of three years for their chance at a dead person's organ. The third option is to receive a kidney from a living donor—usually, though not always, a family member, spouse, or friend.

Doctors agree that, where possible, this latter option is by far the best. Because dialysis machines cannot filter the blood with the same degree of precision as healthy kidneys, and because the process itself is both mentally and physically draining, dialysis offers most people a frankly lousy quality of life. And transplants from living donors are statistically far more successful than those from cadaveric donors—perhaps because they haven't been damaged by brain death and cold storage, perhaps for other, more elusive reasons.

And so, it seemed to me, our choice was clear.

We knew Ana's kidneys were failing, but we didn't know how fast. Three months before her last nephrons sputtered out, her doctor told us he thought we still had two years. My intuition told me otherwise, and I began the series of tests given to potential donors—but not quickly enough. Nauseous, bloated, and confused from the toxin build-up, Ana was forced to spend eight weeks on dialysis before my tests were complete. The process required her to undergo two separate surgical procedures, and left her traumatized, depressed, and weak. And so transplantation day, when it finally arrived, felt like a tremendous victory. Although we should have known better, we saw it, I think, as the end of our journey.

It wasn't. It was the beginning.

ONE

Yesterday a nurse wheeled Ana off for a treatment to prevent her from getting the kind of pneumonia people with AIDS get, now that the doctors have made her susceptible to it. She's on high doses of three drugs that suppress the immune system—standard procedure, after a transplant. I was still in the hospital then, in the bed next to hers, and I lay there and cried.

But when she came back she told me that all through the session, breathing in the antibiotic mist, she'd let herself be taken away by her hawk, her spirit guide, *el gavilán*. He carried her all over Puerto Rico, from the top of El Yunque, the rainforest where tiny wild strawberries hide between orchids and plumes of towering fern, through Bayamón, where she stopped in to visit at her sister's busy little bicycle shop. They passed through Vega Baja, where she saw her great aunt Nina Fe in the turquoise and yellow *casita* she's lived in for almost all of her 101 years, through Fajardo and Hato Rey, Manatí and Mayaguez, and then, when it was time for Ana's treatment to end, the hawk set her back down at California Pacific Medical Center in San Francisco.

Ana's body is damaged from twenty-six years of diabetes, and from all the years when she didn't take care of herself—when she smoked, drank, never checked her blood sugar. She still loves to eat the Puerto Rican way: white rice, fried meats, and strong sweet coffee, not a vegetable in sight. But she is resonant with faith, solid and strong and magnificent with faith. She is visited regularly by her brother, mother, and grandmother—all dead;

on the day of the surgery, she told me, she saw all three of them, waltzing triumphantly beside her hospital bed. She keeps a white candle burning for *paz*, not world peace but the more personal kind: serenity, harmony, kindness in our home. As a teenager she spent several years in theology school; now she treasures with equal fervor her reproduced artifacts from the Taínos, the Indians who lived in Puerto Rico until the Spaniards slaughtered them, and her ceramic figurine of St. Lucia offering forth her two eyes on a plate. Her faith is not particular; she believes in Jesus, but not in any specific church's version of him, and she doesn't pray, at least not in the usual sense. She simply feels; she *knows*. Faith glows through her large, scarred, damaged body; it brings her hawk to her and brings her home again.

This transplant is an act of faith.

And faith is difficult for me; I've always relied more on my mind, my will. I'm comfortable when I have a task to perform; and today, my first day back at home, I assume that my task is to rest, to recover from surgery. That seems tangible enough. I spend most of the day in bed, quilts plumped-up around me, one or both cats purring nearby. I feel almost as if I have the flu, with diarrhea and a malodorous sweat I've never experienced before. I tire quickly, after an hour or two out of bed, showering, cooking, feeding the animals. But I have little pain, just some stiffness in my side. My five-inch scar is neatly covered with Steri-Strip tape; beneath it, the incision has already begun to seal over. I am awed by my body's ability to heal.

But if my task now is to *believe*, as Ana does—here is where I fail. I lie in bed crying, terrified. Is she rejecting the kidney now? Will the transplant end here? We've met people who lost the new kidney within the first week; it's not common, but it happens. It could happen to her.

Alison calls to tell me she's talked to a psychic who said there would be a "glitch" for Ana after the surgery, but then everything would be all right. I cling to this as my only external reason to hope. I tell Ana about it, crying, and she says, "I know that. I *know* everything will be all right."

I lie in bed and think of Ana's body, tracing it in my mind, moving my eyes and lips over her. Her broad forehead, fine black hair, squirrel-cheeks, plump lips that catch and hold me; her neck, which I love to kiss, tickling her like a baby until she laughs and tries to duck away. Her neck, *cuello* in Spanish, which we transform to *pollo*, chicken, and then *pollito*, little chicken, in our word play. Then her shoulders, her barely furred armpits, the wide back she adores having scratched—*mi changuita*, I call her then, my little monkey, and she makes ecstatic monkey sounds as I rasp my fingernails over her dry skin. Her breasts, heavy and ripe, their large nipples like pink eyes, the moisture they trap beneath them—by the time I reach her breasts, here in our bed without her, I am always crying.

I play music I taped before we met, trying to remember the time before she grew solid and sturdy as a redwood tree right in the center of my life.

I open a book of poetry, Li-Young Lee's *Rose,* and read:

O, to take what we love inside,
to carry within us an orchard, to eat
not only the skin, but the shade,
not only the sugar, but the days . . .

The poem is about faith, about embracing everything. I know there is no way to reach the life I hope for without holding this entire orchard inside me, "not only the skin, but the shade." And I am grateful to be healing so quickly; I'd expected far more pain. Yet I feel so utterly stripped of defenses, the space between laughing and crying shifted closer than ever.

I play music Ana taped for me, romantic *baladas. "Cómo quisiera poder vivir sin aire,"* a man's voice sings. *"Cómo quisiera poder vivir sin ti."* How much he longs to be able to live without air, or without the one he loves, he declares—as if they were one and the same thing. Ana's calico cat, the one we call La Manchada (or, with a Puerto Rican accent, La Manchá), the stained one, stays near me, washing, purring, stretching out her long, elegant orange paws with their white boots and black inkstains.

I open a newspaper, read the personal ads. This is, after all, the 1990s; relationships are as easy to find as computers or recliners or anything else one might go shopping for—or so the ads imply. I see several ads I might answer if I were single; I imagine placing one myself, sometime in the distant future, after Ana has died, after I've mourned. This is crazy—a diversionary tactic. I tell myself to think instead about the richness of our love, how it has deepened and changed me, how lucky Ana and I are—no matter what happens, no matter when—to have loved each other this way. But I'm crying again.

I drink strong fresh ginger tea with honey and lemon, trying to soothe my colicky stomach; I run back and forth to the toilet. When I fall asleep again I dream that Ana and I are in Santa Fe; I've parked close to the edge of a cliff and Ana, thinking to steer us out of danger, drives the car over the cliff instead. And yet, miraculously, we are unhurt, even the vehicle undamaged.

☙

Ana's serum creatinine should drop. That would mean that my kidney was cleaning her blood, that her body wasn't rejecting it. Instead, it rises. Normal levels are between .75 and 1.5; hers was up to 6 or 7 at its highest point, then fell to 1.9 by Day 3 post-transplant. Then it started going up again, and hasn't stopped. Is this a rejection? An adjustment period? Or is it Cyclosporine toxicity? Ironically, Cyclosporine, the main drug used to prevent organ rejection, is itself toxic to the kidneys, so a very delicate balance must be achieved: too little, and the kidney is lost; too much, and it's ruined.

The doctors put forth one theory, then another, then they start Ana on high-dose IV steroids—the first line of attack against rejection. We wait.

After three days alone at home, I feel well enough to drive myself to the hospital to visit Ana. But I stop first at the university library, where, slouched in a chair, my handbag propped up to cushion my sore side, I read as many transplant journals as I can find. I fill pages with notes, reassured by what I find, not so much by any one article as by the sheer bulk of the literature. I also see very clearly just how imperfect, how incomplete, the doctors' knowledge is.

"I read about testing the urine for IL-2 and IL-6 levels to distinguish between rejection and Cyclosporine toxicity," I venture later, when the doctor comes by for rounds. It's Dr. Lucca, a tall, brusque, handsome man in his forties. He was the doctor we saw when we first went to the transplant center to be evaluated, seven months ago, when all the doctors were saying Ana's kidneys wouldn't fail for another two years or more, and he was cool to us then. We were strangers; he might never see us again. Now that we're under his care he's warmed up only slightly.

"That's experimental. We don't do that here," he responds again and again as I go down my page of notes. Finally he sighs wearily. "Look, it's easy enough to write up a study, but that's not *proof*. Here we wait until techniques have been established, refined."

"What about fish oil?" I ask. It's the last note on my page. Several studies had suggested that people taking fish oil capsules experienced less organ rejection, along with various other benefits including lowered blood pressure.

He gives me a surprised nod. "I like fish oil, myself. A lot of the doctors on staff here don't, but I do. I recommend it to my patients with chronic rejection."

"But the article I read said the benefit is probably greatest if it's started soon after transplant."

"Well, yes, it probably is," the doctor concedes.

"Would that be something I could just go out and buy? Or you could prescribe for her?"

"Sure, you can buy it. All the drugstores have it. But if you want to do it right," he adds helpfully, "look for MAX-EPA brand. That's the brand they tested in the European studies."

The fish oil capsules are huge, and smell slightly fishy. The dose is six per day, two with each meal. If I'd suggested them to Ana on my own, she'd never take them; she's overwhelmed enough already with all the pills. But the doctor's blessing has impressed her; she swallows them like magic. "Can't hurt," we repeat to each other like a mantra. "They can't hurt."

But the rejection episode, if it is one, doesn't turn around. For a day or two on the steroids her creatinine hovers stable; then it starts creeping up again. They begin testing it two, three times a day. 2.6, 2.8, 3.0. 3.1 . . . They'd been talking about discharging her soon; now there's no question of that. "If we give you the OKT3, you'll be in here at least another ten days," Helena, the transplant coordinator, warns one afternoon. She's a tall, well-dressed, haughty woman who always speaks in motion, flinging her comments back over her shoulder as she walks off down the hall. She never greets Ana or tells us the results of the latest tests; she just writes on the chart on Ana's door, turns on her heel and hurries off.

Apparently it's been decided, then. Ana will be given OKT3, the drug the doctors refer to as the "big guns": the super-duper heavy-duty anti-rejection drug, a monoclonal antibody fashioned, somehow, from the immune systems of mice. It's a ten-day treatment, at a cost, we learn later, of thirteen hundred dollars a day. Roger, the liver-transplant patient in the next room, got his first infusion yesterday and went through violent tremors for at least an hour afterward—one of the common side effects, we've been told. Later in the afternoon he emerged from his room, weak and shaking. "It wasn't that bad, really it wasn't," he told us. His grin was not convincing.

The OKT3 will target her T-cells, those same cells that people with AIDS all over the world are so desperate to increase. Those critical immune system cells that, now, are attacking the kidney they see as foreign.

"Will this drug actually lower her T-cell count?" I ask Dr. Lucca, primed by my years in AIDS education.

"Oh, yes," he responds cheerfully. "Her T-cell count will go down to almost zero."

How eerie, how brutally ironic this seems. Ana has already developed esophageal thrush, an AIDS-related condition common among people with HIV. After over a decade of watching friends and co-workers die because their immune systems failed, it's hard for me to bear the thought that the doctors are, essentially, giving Ana AIDS. They're willfully decimating one of the few parts of her body that is still strong.

Yet I know too that it was AIDS work that prepared me to survive this transplant, AIDS that showed me how people bear their lovers' illnesses; I'd have felt too sorry for myself otherwise, too uniquely cursed, as if I were the only person in the world to have to deal with a seriously ill partner at age thirty-three.

The day of Ana's first OKT3 infusion I arrive at the hospital with all my effort aimed toward strength, composure. But Ana's bed is empty; they've taken her off for another anti-pneumonia treatment.

"Hey, howya doin'?" Roger, the liver transplant patient, greets me. He's up and walking around, looks better today; I burst into tears and he tries awkwardly to comfort me. "It's not that bad. She's gonna be fine."

I nod, wipe my face with my sleeve. Roger always seems so patient. He's upbeat and affable, an easygoing guy in his late forties. I don't know what he does in his life outside this hospital, but I suspect he manages a lot of people, or a lot of money, and does it very well. "We've got our whole lives ahead of us," he says over and over, to Ana, to me, to anyone who asks.

One of Ana's co-workers is there waiting for me; Ana had asked him to stay, not wanting me to arrive to an empty room. Bob had a cancerous lung removed ten years ago; recently, in a car accident, he fractured several ribs. *What impossibly fragile creatures we are,* I think, and begin to cry again.

This won't do. This is not acceptable. So I pull out my last resort: strength and composure in a tablet—one of the Valium tablets Ana used to take for her leg cramps, which grew agonizing as her kidneys failed. I haven't taken a pill to calm myself down since I was about fifteen, but it works as well now as it did then; it's eerie how well it works. By the time they wheel Ana back I'm frighteningly calm.

The OKT3 is a tiny vial of clear liquid. It looks just like water, or IV solution, or the DHPG they give her daily as a prophylactic antiviral, or, for that matter, the new clear cola on the market. I hold Ana's hand as the doctor slowly pushes in the plunger. He'll stay here in the room for a while afterward; they always do, to see how the patient reacts. He waits; we wait. But nothing happens. Ana goes through none of the ferocious chills or vomiting we've been told about. Instead, lulled by the Benadril they pre-medicated her with, she sleeps. Her Cuban friend José, who came without having been called (she'd called him with her mind, Ana said; she'd asked Adrian, her dead brother, to bring him here), sits in the corner like an owl, meditating, his eyes closed. And I nod and droop, weak with Valium and relief.

⁂

I want to be less fearful, but I don't know how to get there. Pleading with a god I'm not sure I believe in doesn't seem to work. Friends can't help either; there's no one I want to hug except Ana, and no one whose words can reach me through this terror. I write in my journal:

People go through these terrible things, these failed surgeries and attempts. People watch their lovers die. I am not the first person to go through any of this; usually that kind of thinking allows me to pull back— doesn't console me, exactly, but distances me. Yet to think of these things with Ana feels absolutely unbearable, absolutely not within the realm of things which can be borne.

If friends can't help, help has to come from inside. I have to go inside myself. If there's a single grain of faith in me, I have to find it and focus on that.

Before the surgery I'd read books on guided visualization. Preparing myself ahead of time, I'd pictured my body directing the blood flow away from my kidney when the surgeon began to cut, and maybe it had worked; in any event, the doctor told me afterward that I'd bled very little. Now I try to use that technique with my fear. Closing my eyes, I try to go inside my chest, the dark tight center of me.

My powers of visualization aren't as good as Ana's, but I'm able to imagine myself in a dark area that looks like our backyard. It's too dark, in fact, so I imagine up a flashlight. I think of my fears as mushrooms, the ones we're always uprooting from the shady parts of the yard so the dogs won't eat them and be poisoned; I conjure up a plastic Safeway bag and go through the yard with my flashlight, collecting mushrooms/fears until the bag is full. They'll grow there again, I know: mushrooms have spores; you can never get them all. But I see myself tying the plastic bag tightly shut, and when I open my eyes again, in some crazy way I feel better.

Later Ana tells me that before the OKT3 treatment she took another journey with her *gavilán*. Together they traveled, not through Puerto Rico this time but through her body, deeper and deeper along the canals of the blood. "You have to find my immune system, shut it off," she urged the hawk, and he pushed farther and farther through the dark swirls of her organs until he found the switch and pressed it down. "We did it," she promises me. *"El gavilán lo apagó."*

❧

The days settle into a new rhythm. I sleep as late as I can, spend an aimless morning reading whatever's lying around the house—part of the newspaper, the middle of this or that novel; I can't concentrate long enough to read anything start to finish. Then I pack a picnic, sandwiches and fruit, and head off to the hospital around 1:00 or 2:00. My incision itches, but not intolerably; the nerves in the right lower portion of my belly are bruised, making my skin oversensitive, as if it were sunburned. Apart from that I feel fine, not even stiff any more.

And I, who have always hated hospitals, have now learned to sit in Ana's room for six, seven, eight hours, all through the afternoon and evening. I squinch up against her, sharing her hospital bed; we chat with friends who call or come by, listen to music, watch a little TV, stroll the corridors, talk with the nurses and other patients. She's made friends with a few of them: Roger, of course, and also Luis, the young Puerto Rican on the other side whose brother gave him a kidney. She knows which nurses have children, where they live, what to joke about with them; since she's diabetic, she gives them the candy her co-workers send. Our friends have brought and sent so many flowers that we give some of those away, too. I remember again that this is one of the things I love about Ana: the way she pays attention to the people around her, starts up a community on the spot. I'm getting to know the daily life of this ward now, our own temporary small town.

There's another young Latino man in a room down the hall, a recent kidney transplant; we've tried to make friends with him on our walks, but he doesn't seem to want to talk. One night, sitting in the little lounge area halfway around the maze-like corridor, we talk with two elderly Mexicans who turn out to be his parents. They're from the countryside outside Guanajuato, transported here as if from a different world. The man wears a big straw hat; his large, rough hands are farmer's hands. The woman clutches a woven shawl around her, her body shapeless inside it, slack and crumpled. They have eleven children, they tell us; the young man in the room is their youngest *varon*, male child. He is twenty-one.

"What happened to his kidneys?" I ask in Spanish.

The old man is the one who speaks. "He was working in the lettuce. They found him in the field, bleeding from his nose and mouth. He was in a coma for nine days. We thought he was going to die."

"From the pesticides? Here in the U.S.?" I ask, shocked. Ana nods in confirmation. "Is that what the doctors said it was?"

"*Cerca de Fresno*. Near Fresno. He was working in the lettuce," the old man repeats, sadly.

We try to reassure the old couple. "This is a very good hospital. Kidney transplants can last a long time now."

"*Gracias*," they nod graciously. "*Gracias*."

One of their other children, a twenty-four-year-old daughter, donated the kidney. "I gave a kidney to my friend, too. Ten days ago," I explain, pulling up my T-shirt to show off my incision. Now the woman's face becomes animated; she clutches her husband's sleeve with one hand, moves the other hand gingerly toward me. "*Qué bueno, qué bueno,*" she murmurs. "*¿Pero no le duele?*"

"*Ya no. Está casi sano ya.*" *It doesn't hurt; it's almost healed.* I think of something else then, a misconception a few of my friends had mentioned. "Some people say that someone who gives a kidney can't have children, but that's not true. Even with one kidney, that's no problem," I tell her in Spanish.

The woman straightens her shoulders now, and I see that she is not, after all, so old. "*¿Es cierto?*" she asks Ana eagerly, searching her face for confirmation.

"*Sí, sí. Su hija todavía puede tener hijos,*" we assure her. *Your daughter can still have children.*

"*Ay, ¡qué bueno que me hayan dicho eso!*" *How wonderful that you've told me that.* She looks joyful, relieved. I realize there's been no one else she could talk to, no one she could ask.

Later my friend Na'ama says, "That's why it's so important to buy organic produce. It's not just because it's better for *us;* it's so the people who pick the crops won't have to be poisoned."

And she adds, "People working in the fields don't know how dangerous those chemicals are. I've heard sometimes they take the empty pesticide buckets, use them to carry drinking water."

Months after this, in a bookstore, I'll leaf through a book about migrant workers. Among the photos, I'll see one of a young Latina girl in a cucumber field; half-hidden in the lush green leaves, she's taking a break, eating a cucumber. The caption beneath the photo reveals that the field had been sprayed with pesticides the day before. Another page quotes a social worker who confirms that kidney failure is common among the migrant workers. "Many are on dialysis by age forty-five," she says.

❧

One night Ana calls me around midnight, an hour after I left her dozing in her hospital bed. She's had a nightmare, she's near-hysterical; she doesn't even remember what she dreamed, just the feeling of it: *Terror. Loss of control.*

"It's the Imuran," the nurse assures her. One of the immunosuppressants sometimes causes nightmares; they usually give it to patients in the morning, for just that reason, but through some mishap Ana has been getting her dose at dinnertime.

But knowing there's an explanation helps only a little. Ana sounds more frightened, more lost than I've ever heard her. Words feel so useless; they can't reach down into the well of fear where she's fallen.

"Do you want me to come back over there? I could be there in half an hour, spend the night with you there," I offer, fighting off my tiredness.

"No, no, you need your sleep. I'll be fine," she says, making herself sound stronger now, as if she's ready to get off the phone. I don't buy it.

"I love you." I drop my words down to her like coins. "This is just from the pills. You'll feel better in the morning. It's going to pass. I love you."

And then I think to ask, "Where is your hawk, *el gavilán?* Can he help you through this?"

Her voice is blind with despair. "I tried that. I can't find him."

So I go back to trying to soothe, to cradle her with my disembodied voice. Finally around 1:00 she says she thinks she really will be able to go back to sleep now, the sleeping pill the nurse gave her is starting to work. Reluctantly, I put down the phone. We each travel alone through that dark country, sleep.

Ana has a roommate now: Carmen, a forty-three-year-old Chicana who just got her second kidney transplant. The first one lasted her four years.

"Three good years," she tells us. "The fourth year I had to go back on dialysis. One of my nephews came over with his kids; I knew the baby had a cold, but I couldn't tell them to take her home. So I got sick from that, and it ruined the kidney."

Ana tells me fiercely, "I won't make that mistake. I'll go to work wearing a mask if I have to. I won't let anyone with a cold into the house."

But the doctors have a different explanation for Carmen's second kidney failure. "Chronic rejection," they call it. And it grows clear to us that Carmen's understanding of her situation isn't terribly sophisticated. Several mornings in a row Ana finds Carmen's anti-fungal lozenges on the bathroom floor. "Do you know what these are for?" she confronts her, finally.

"No," Carmen admits.

"They're so you won't get white stuff on your tongue. You know, the drugs you're taking lower your immune system, so your body won't attack the kidney. That means you can get other problems. You know, like when you get a yeast infection? That white stuff is the same thing, only in your mouth. These *pastillitas* keep it from taking over."

Carmen nods, impressed. She's been diabetic for twenty-five years, the same length of time as Ana, but when her family comes to visit they bring her a regular soda instead of a diet one.

"You know what that soda does to you?" Ana grills her afterward. "It raises your blood sugar! That's why you have all those sores that won't heal. Tell them to bring you diet next time."

And Carmen can hardly see, her eyes have gotten so bad from the diabetes. Sometimes she doesn't recognize Ana when she comes back into the room after a walk in the hallway; how can she possibly see the readings on her glucometer? "Tell them to get you one of those glucometers with real big numbers," Ana instructs. "If you keep your sugar lower, your vision will be clearer, too."

And, later, "You've had children; you know how much care a baby needs. You have to think of that kidney like a new baby. You have to eat right, take your medicine, do everything the doctors tell you so your baby can be strong and healthy."

"Oh," says Carmen, intrigued by this new perspective. "*Tienes razón.*"

And I'm thinking, *They invest a hundred thousand bucks in a transplant for this woman, it fails and they do it a second time, and they don't even bother to make sure she knows what she has to do, and why? They can't throw in a few hundred more for some sessions with a social worker or a health educator, preferably a Latina, who could do an assessment and work with her on this stuff?*

And I'm also thinking, *If this kind of thing is common, that goes a long way toward explaining why the stats aren't better. Ana knows what she's doing. She's bound to do much better than average.*

It's the first time I've felt optimistic.

⟨⟩

Finally, twenty days after our surgery, the doctors tell us Ana can go home.

This is her second leave-taking. The first time, a few days after starting the ten-day course of OKT3, she left the hospital for one night. The doctors said she could come back every day for the infusion; the insurance companies pressure them to send patients home as soon as possible, they explained. On our way out Ana gave Roger a shiny Mylar "Get Well Soon" balloon one of her friends had brought.

It was a sunny afternoon, slightly breezy. Ana sat on our deck with the dogs and cats clustered around her; I brought her food, drink, pills, a sweater. I had thought I'd recovered already, but now, having to care for her as well as myself, I was exhausted.

By nighttime she had a fever of 101°, and she was so weak she could barely make it up the stairs to our bedroom. In the morning, when I brought her in to the hospital, the doctors admitted her. Infection, they said. Septicemia. It could be from the central line they'd put in her chest; they'd take the line out, clean her up and put in a new one, give her more Benadril along with the antibiotics she was allergic to. At first they said they'd discontinue the OKT3, she didn't need it any more, she was no longer in rejection; but the next afternoon when I arrive they're giving it to her again, the familiar tiny vial dripping ever so slowly into her new central line.

"Doesn't that make it harder for her body to fight the infection?" I ask.

"Yes, but we decided to push the envelope," Dr. Lucca says.

Although I know it's a common expression, his use of the jargon chills me. To him, I think, Ana is just a statistic, another number added or deleted from the hospital's success rosters. The transplant center at this hospital is ranked among the best in the country. And I know the doctors here have treated thousands of patients, but sometimes I have the feeling they're just guessing, experimenting, trying out this or that the way a cook might add a pinch of spice to a new dish—just as if no one's life depended on it.

The following week, when he gets discharged, Roger gives Ana back her balloon. As he slowly changes from hospital gown to street clothes, seated on his bed with the curtain pulled around him, I talk briefly with his wife. She's about fifteen years older than me, a blonde suburbanite, perky and chic; I'm astonished by the kinship I feel with her, this woman with whom, on the old surface of our lives, I have so little in common. I hadn't known it would be like this, this wartime camaraderie.

So now Ana is coming home for the second time. I bring bags of Pepperidge Farm cookies for all the nurses; we exchange hugs. "I want to buy your book of poetry when it comes out!" one insists, thrusting her address into my hand; Ana must have been bragging about me again. I bring up a wheelchair from the lobby and she perches on it, beatific, loaded down with bags: clothing, toiletries, medications, the portable cd player, her "Super-Teddy" teddy bear with his Velcro Superman cape. We leave the latest bouquet of flowers at the nurses' station, wheel gaily off.

Outside, we step back into the world: honking maneuvering cars, people trotting their dogs across the street. It's the last day of May, sunny, but with the brisk chill of ocean fog making its way toward us. We step back into our lives.

TWO

A friend who had her first baby two months ago writes, "I could never have imagined what this would be like. It's so much more exhausting than I would have thought, but there's also so much more joy." And in a sense that's what it's like now for me too, four weeks after the transplant—so much better, and so much harder, than I could have imagined. In the shower I soap Ana up, not because I have to any longer, as I did in the months before the transplant—when she was too weak, too overcome by body ache to bathe herself—but because it's another way to touch her. I stroke her incision, then mine, trying to make myself believe the surgery really happened, that my kidney is there inside her now, that that's why she feels better. *Parece mentira*, they say in Spanish, *it seems like a lie*, that unreal.

And she *does* feel better. "A hundred percent," she tells everyone who asks. "I feel like I've been reborn."

I look at scraps of poetry I wrote in the months before the surgery and remember the leaden weight I felt then, the depth of grief and despair, and I see that things *are* different now. I think, *It's time to get my life back, after so many months when I could barely think of what I felt or wanted, there was no room; Ana's needs were too great, my sadness was too great.* I think, *It's time for Ana and me to get our relationship back, the joy of it, beyond these narrow roles of patient and caretaker.* And yet—

"When can you know you're home free, that her body's accepted the kidney?" friends ask. "Never." "How much longer does she have to take the drugs that suppress her immune system?" "For the rest of her life." "Oh," they say. The miracle stops here. And yet—

At a Kidney Foundation dinner honoring organ donors we see a videotape from the last Transplant Games, an Olympics-type event for transplant recipients. Watching the sun-dappled scenes, everyone running and jumping, swimming and hugging and laughing, I imagine each of these athletes as they once must have been, as Ana was in February—pale, exhausted, her life force visibly flickering as if it might soon go out. The videotape was made by the company that manufactures Cyclosporine, but for a moment I leave cynicism aside. They call organ donation "the gift of life," and watching this tape I can see why.

And yet Ana's creatinine still isn't where it should be, and it has risen, not fallen, with each of the last four blood tests. This is the same trend the doctors called rejection last time, treated with the "big guns"; now they tell us not to be concerned, sometimes the numbers take a while to stabilize. What's the difference between last time and this time? How do they differentiate between rejection and "just taking a while"? Sometimes they do kidney biopsies, but the kidney has burrowed so deep inside Ana that that would be difficult in her case. "That little rascal, he's made a home for himself in there," the surgeon teases. So we wait.

"I trust the doctors totally—in terms of their commitment to keeping you alive," says Dorey, a woman in our transplant support group whose husband is on the list for a new liver. "Where I don't trust them is in their commitment to your *quality* of life." And that makes sense to me. But the truth is, I don't trust them at all.

And yet I *have* to trust them.

I have to learn to live with a different balance now, a different level of precariousness in my world—and, as with most lessons, I'm resisting it like hell.

I am frightened, now, to give up living as if in crisis, because no one can promise me the crisis is over, or for how long.

⊱⚭⊰

All through the long winter, as Ana's kidneys failed, we'd talked about getting two kittens in the spring. And now, the week after her hospital release, she wants to go by the animal shelter. "Just to look," she insists, and I, who should know better, go along with it.

It's early June, the height of kitten season, and there are dozens of them in the shelter's dirty, stinking main room, huddled together in their cages, cowering at the endless background noise of barking dogs. Of course we can't resist; the kittens are so cute, and they look so miserable. We leave with two of them, a fuzzy blue-eyed Siamese mix and a miniature brown-striped green-eyed tiger we christen Kiwi, for her coloring.

But the new members of our family are very small and very demanding. Chico, the blue-eyed little boy, has diarrhea, which we learn about on the way home from the shelter when he shits all over Ana's leg. We attribute it to nerves, though, and at first the kittens seem happy and healthy enough, eating, playing, curling up together behind our bed. But they cry whenever we leave the room, and Kiwi soon scales the two-foot gate in the doorway and begins following us through the rest of the house, mewing like a little wraith, astonishingly loud for such a tiny creature.

We begin to carry them everywhere we go—into the kitchen, the living room, the garden. But Chico's diarrhea is a worsening problem. Since he's the fuzzy one, the thick, viscous shit sticks to his fur, covering his little tail and hind legs; we try to clean him, but he keeps shitting and soon develops an abscess on his tail. The vet prescribes droppersful of a thick banana-flavored medicine, but it doesn't seem to help; neither does our attempt to switch him from canned to dry food. He won't eat the dry food; after a while he won't eat at all.

I feel overwhelmed, burdened. I'm taking care of the kittens, of course, as well as caring for Ana and myself. I catch myself thinking, "In a month they'll be bigger, healthier, less demanding. I just have to get through the month." Then I notice what I'm doing, and exhaustion and resentment surge up in me; for so many months of Ana's illness I'd lived like that, just steeling myself to get through.

It's when Ana hears me sobbing on the phone to a friend that she finally mouths to me, "Let's take them back." But we can't bear to return them to the hellhole we got them from, so I call all over trying to find a decent shelter with room for them. Ana doesn't even want to touch or look at them that night; she's detaching, she says. But I wake up at 3:00 A.M., worried about Chico; he's barely eaten since we switched him to dry food, and with all the diarrhea he must be dehydrated. I run downstairs naked to give him some canned food, and he gums it around a little, tiny and stinking, purring up a storm.

By morning he looks even worse. He can barely move, though he still purrs when I stroke his knobby little spine. "There's no way the shelter will take him in this condition. His fever's so high it doesn't even register. I'd say his prognosis is 'guarded,' less than a 50 percent chance—and that's if we treat him aggressively, which will cost you a few hundred dollars, at least," says the shelter vet.

"It would certainly be a humane option," he adds, "to put him to sleep."

I hesitate, crying. Ana is at the transplant clinic a few blocks away, awaiting her checkup; I have to make this decision alone.

"That's what I would do," the vet says.

And that's what I do.

Kiwi, who has ridden in on my shoulder, looks calmly toward her future with those piercing green eyes of hers. The vet assures me that there's nothing else, nothing different we could have done for Chico; he would have gotten sick whether we'd adopted him or not. Ana says later that he's gone to kitten heaven. Yet the sadness stays with me—how this ill-timed gesture we made toward new life has ended, instead, in death.

Ana has been on two blood pressure medications since she left the hospital, plus a diuretic and an angina medication. But nothing seems to work. Normal blood pressure is 125 over 75; she's getting readings like 180 over 100. Right after she takes the Procardia in the morning her pressure is down a little, but still not enough, maybe 165 over 95. We know that prolonged high blood pressure will damage the kidney; in fact, it's a major cause of renal failure. And so soon after the transplant anything that isn't working "right," anything that reminds us of how little control we really have, is terrifying.

We call the transplant service doctor on call; he suggests taking the Procardia twice a day. Ana tries it for a few days, but her readings are still high. We call back. "Okay," he says, "Try quadrupling it, then. Take two in the morning, two at night."

The new regimen proves more effective. Ana starts getting readings like 140 over 80, sometimes even lower, 120 over 75, 110 over 70. We're relieved. Things are in control again. But the new prescription complicates things with her HMO; Ana runs out of the Procardia four times faster now, of course, and when we try to pick up her refill the computer won't let us.

"It says 'refill too soon,'" the pharmacist tells me.

"But they quadrupled her dose. The new prescription was faxed here."

"Well, somebody must not have keyed it in right," he shrugs.

Ana is waiting in the car, and I'm desperate. In this moment the Procardia seems to me her lifeline. "Can you sell me some, say, a week's worth, that I can pay for out-of-pocket? Until the insurance gets straightened out?"

"Yeah, I guess I can do that. As long as we have a copy of her prescription on file. How many do you need, seven?"

"No, I need *twenty-eight*. She's on four a day now. That's why we ran out."

He raises an eyebrow. "That'll cost over a hundred dollars."

"Look." I'm near tears. "My partner just had a kidney transplant. The medications she's on now are to keep her *alive*." I enunciate with extreme care. "We will do whatever we have to do to get them."

So I pay the money; someday, maybe, her insurance company will reimburse me. The important thing is that we have the medication she needs.

☙

Dorey calls to read me the flyer for the new support group she and I are starting: a group for "caregivers"—spouses, friends, family—of people pre- and post-transplant.

"How's Gene?" I ask her. "Any new developments?"

"We saw the doctor yesterday. He's number ten on the liver list, but he's been number ten for four months."

It's hard to know what to say. Roger had told us he'd been number one on the liver transplant list for months; he kept getting passed over when livers became available, because other people were sicker than he was.

"Fourth of July weekend is coming up," I offer, hopefully. It's a ghoulish joke in the support group—but not entirely a joke; people waiting for transplants have better luck on holiday weekends, when the rest of the world is out drinking too much and getting into car wrecks.

"Yeah," Dorey agrees. "We asked the doctor if we could go away that weekend, and he said 'Hmmm—you're number ten on the list? Sure, no problem.'"

"Good news and bad news."

"Right. Also, Gene told the doctor yesterday that for the first time he viscerally feels—not just knows intellectually, but *feels*—that he's dying. The doctor just said, 'Mmmm-hmmm.'"

"Is that how he experiences it?" I ask, shocked. "Like he's dying?"

And Dorey says quietly, "He feels a little worse each day."

I know what that's like, I think; for months I watched Ana going through the same thing. And yet for the first time, hearing Dorey's words, I really feel how different Dorey's situation is from mine. A transplant is the only way Gene can stay alive. He'll die without one, and he'll die if he doesn't get one soon enough. There's no dialysis when your liver fails.

Later Ana and I talk about this, reflecting back on the months of her kidney failure, weeks when she ate nothing but toast and applesauce and found it hard to stomach even that. We're eating the Greek salad I've made for our dinner. "We went through so much," I say. "But we were dealing with how much longer you could keep up your spirit, your *will* to live, when the quality of your life was so poor. We never had to wonder whether you would survive long enough to get the transplant."

In the grocery store this morning, thumbing through *People Magazine* as I waited in line, I read about Christopher Reeve, the Superman star. He's forty-two, a year older than Ana; his wife, Dana, whom I liked because she looked like a regular person in the picture, is thirty-four, a year older than me. He fell off a horse a week ago, and it appears he'll be permanently paralyzed from the neck down. *What is his wife thinking?* I wondered. She's young; they have a small child, her first. Of course she'll stay with him through the initial crisis, but in the long term, will she stick it out? *Should* she? Can there be any kind of life for her with him now, beyond self-sacrifice? Is there a level of disability beyond which it's impossible to sustain real love? Or can it really be enough just to have the one you love alive—no matter what kind of life they have?

Ana and I aren't married, of course; society doesn't offer us that option. But I knew about her health problems from early on; I chose this life with her, "in sickness and in health." And people whose partners are healthy seem unable, so often, to understand my life; they act as if my being with Ana—my giving her the kidney, in particular—makes me some kind of Mother Teresa. The truth is I'm with Ana because she makes me happy, because I'm crazy in love with her, even now, maybe especially now.

For years I had worried about how it would be when her health worsened, as we both knew it would. I'd feared my passion wouldn't survive; I'd wondered whether I'd end up staying with her out of a sense of obligation, whether I'd stay at all. In fact, through the hardest days I've been shocked by the constancy of my love, the selfish, stubborn, unquenchable force of my desire. At Ana's weakest point I had to dress and undress her; even that degree of motion was too much for her. And yet it was still *her* body I touched, that lush wild body that had rippled through so many earthquakes in my mouth, my hands. She couldn't respond to me at all then, and I cried with wanting her. It would have been easier then if I could have wanted her less.

In this moment Ana looks so robust, voraciously spearing olives and feta cheese with her fork, her plump cheeks flushed with color. Less than four months ago her skin was a pasty gray; her eyes were dull, her body aches so bad she couldn't lift her arms without my help. I look at her now and think, *How can I ever feel dissatisfied?* This miracle, this one right here in front of me, this should last me a lifetime. *Dayenu*, as we say during Passover Seder, naming each small cause for gratitude—telling God that just that one, that one alone, would have been enough.

And yet it's not enough. Ana's groin is numb, the nerves bruised from her surgery; when I try to touch her there it prickles and stings. "It should be better in three months," the surgeon tells us. "Nerves are slow to heal; it could be six," a doctor friend says. I've waited so long for us to be able to make love again, for us to come together as we used to, with passion as well as tenderness. And so, in spite of all our blessings, I cry still from frustration, not joy.

"You've been so patient," Ana tells me, her eyes filling too.

"No, I haven't been patient at all; I've been impatient, but for a long time," I say, and she has to laugh because it's true.

⌘

On Wednesday nights we perform the pillbox ritual, an act of faith as much as any other. Ana takes hundreds of pills each week. Large and small, round and oblong, bright and dull, we place them into the four neat slots for each day, the twenty-eight slots for the week. We sit on the bed surrounded by bottles, Ana shaking, counting, plinking the pills out, while I snip open the endless foil-sealed packets of Cyclosporine. They're enormous dusty-pink capsules, reeking of skunk, dominating the pillbox with their heft; Ana's current dose is seventeen of them per day. This is the one-time wonder drug that revolutionized organ transplantation, making rejection far less frequent, but now they've been around a while—ten years?—and their failings, too, have become all too clear. In addition to being toxic to the kidneys, they raise the blood pressure so dramatically that even people who weren't hypertensive before become so on Cyclosporine. They also cost about ten bucks each, so at this dosage, I've figured out, a three-month supply runs close to fifteen thousand dollars.

In the Transplant Games video a mother of one of the young athletes gushed into the camera, "And thank you to the Sandoz Corporation for making this wonderful drug, Cyclosporine, which is keeping my daughter alive." It's hard for me to think of them like that, these smelly bullet-shaped pink monstrosities. *These* are what's keeping the woman I love alive? These, and the hundreds of other pills we plunk weekly into her box, seem to me like part of her pact with the devil. After the pills come the foul-tasting antifungal lozenges she lets dissolve in her mouth four times a day, and after that the yellow "swish and swallow" antifungal goop—and still thrush coats her tongue white.

Kyra, our support group leader, tells us she taped a motto above the dresser where she keeps her pills. "This is better than the alternative," it reads. It's a useful phrase.

And these days when we smell skunk on the highway we both call out at once, "Cyclosporine!" Truly, it's the same smell. Then we laugh; we have to laugh.

◈

Seven weeks after the surgery Ana suggests we go to Reno for the weekend. She loves slot machines, and I figure she deserves a treat; anyway, I think, I can just lie by the pool. I'm still out of work on disability, though I feel fine; the transplant surgeon put me down for eight weeks, so I'm taking the time, giving Ana and myself a chance to get accustomed to our new life.

The night before we leave I call my friend Julia, who lives right on our route. Her answering-machine greeting always makes me smile.

"Hannah, can you say 'hello'?" Julia's voice urges, and then two-year-old Hannah's voice, thick with pride, imitates Julia's intonation: "Ha-woh?" Then Julia again, "Hannah, can you say 'Please leave a message'?" and Hannah, "Pweez weev mess-edge," and then the beep. "I know it's last minute," I say, "but we'll be driving through, if you'd like us to stop by . . . "

And Julia calls back later that night, sounding tired, sick—something. "Steve's in the hospital," she tells me. "The doctors don't know what it is yet. Sophie calls it a 'broken brain.'" Sophie, her older daughter, is seven. "On Saturday morning when I woke up he could barely move; his speech was slurred. He's doing better now; they're giving him tons of steroids to bring the inflammation down, but they still don't know what caused it."

"They don't have *any* idea?"

"They went down the list of all the most alarming possibilities first, even the really unlikely ones—leukemia, lymphoma. On Saturday they thought there was only a fifty-fifty chance he'd live. Now that he's responded so dramatically to the steroids, that rules out a lot of things. But I don't know—*they* don't know. They're doing every test known to man, I think," she adds wryly. "But I've been thinking about you, thinking you'd understand."

I'm stunned. Julia visited me a few weeks ago, while Ana was still in the hospital. She brought me a wild rice salad with raisins and pecans, and we sat out on the deck drinking lemonade, and after a while I cried—it was one of the days when the news wasn't good; Ana's creatinine was up again and I was scared. And Julia tried to be sympathetic, but it was clear to me that she just didn't get it then. My good friend, a brilliant poet and child psychologist, infinitely wise with words and children, didn't understand my life at all. "I don't know how you do it," she told me. "I don't think *I* could, if it were Steve. I think I'd leave him."

I was aghast. "Do you really think that?"

"Well, I don't know," she conceded, "but I don't think I'd be as patient as you've been."

I didn't bother to correct her about my patience. I was troubled by what she said; troubled, too, that she couldn't understand why my mood went up or down with each day's hospital report, why I couldn't just treat all this time as a "writing vacation."

"If it were one of my children," she told me, "it would be as if it were happening to me. There'd be no separation there. But with Steve . . . " she shrugged.

"But none of us knows how we'll behave in a situation like this until it happens," I told her. "I would never have known I'd be able to go through this either." And that was true. Years before I'd watched my friends whose lovers had AIDS with a combination of awe and terror, thinking, *I could never be that faithful.*

And now I hear how exhausted and frantic Julia sounds, and how, in the midst of that, she reaches out for hope. "My dad thinks he's going to be okay," she says. Julia's father is a neurologist. "He said some of the possibilities the other doctor told me about were ridiculous. He thinks maybe it's just a weird reaction to one of the viruses Steve had recently, a meningitis."

But she also says, "It feels like my life is never, ever going to be the same."

And I, thinking, *His brain is swollen, his brain is broken,* say, "Well, hopefully it'll turn out to be something relatively minor, and you'll just learn whatever lessons people are supposed to learn from these things and go on like before."

"But I don't *need* to learn any of those lessons," Julia wails. "I really, really think I know those things already."

And I suspect she's wrong, but it doesn't seem useful to say that to her—not now.

We stop to see her, briefly, on our way to Reno. She's rushing to bring Hannah to the hospital. "Steve said he's lonely," she tells us, wonderingly. "He's been crying a lot. It's so unlike him."

"Being in the hospital makes people feel naked, stripped of control," I tell her.

"Oh," says my wise psychologist friend. "Oh, okay." She straps Hannah into her car seat and drives off, and we follow, waving.

Back on the road Ana tells me, "I'm going to keep Steve in my prayers." She hadn't wanted to say that to Julia, who is Jewish, for fear of offending her, but it seems to me like exactly the right thing to say, and to do. I'm struck again by how much her faith offers. What comparable promise could I have made Julia—"I'll keep Steve in my worries?"

Later Ana tells me casually that she sent her hawk, *el gavilán*, to embrace Steve in his hospital bed.

Driving home from Reno we're both hot and tired; the drive takes hours longer than it should have because I take the scenic route through Lake Tahoe, forgetting how slow the winding mountain and lake-edge roads are, not counting on construction work and massive traffic. Finally, on the last stretch of parched hills along Route 80, an hour of dull driving still to go, I begin, silently, to cry. It's the first trip we've ever taken when I feel further from Ana, not closer to her, upon our return.

I'd expected her to be distracted in Reno, to spend hours gambling while I swam or read. But I'd asked her before we left, wanting to prepare myself: "Are you thinking of this trip as just a chance to gamble, or a chance for us to spend time together, too?"

"Both," she'd said.

"So in the morning when we wake up, we'll be able to cuddle? You won't have to race right off to the slot machines?"

"Of course not," she'd said. "Of course we can cuddle."

And so my feelings are hurt the first morning when, upon waking, she pads right over to the TV and turns on the cartoons. *She knows I hate TV!* I fume silently. *But she's getting her life back again, too,* I answer myself. Then, when she looks like she's heading toward the shower, I hear myself saying coldly, "If you're not going to watch that, could you turn it off?" I lie in bed thinking about what I should say instead: *Please turn off the TV and come back here and hold me.* But I don't say that, and Ana, oblivious, says, "I *am* watching it." Which I hear as "Fuck you."

And "cuddling" had, in part, been my code term for making love. I always hoped we'd make love in the mornings, but most especially when we were on a trip, freed from the distractions of the house and animals; and almost always, on past trips, we had.

So now I brood my way down Highway 80, this flat wide swath through the dangerously dry hills. I argue with myself, making angry, wounded accusations in my mind; making retorts to them. It's easy to focus my fury on money; I know Ana lost over a hundred dollars in Reno: not a huge sum, but enough to have taken me away to a nice romantic place for a night instead—*if* that had been her priority, which clearly it wasn't, I think.

On the way home she'd wanted to stop in Sacramento at a stamp shop she'd heard about to get something else for her stamp collection; that stung me, too. Months ago, the day before the surgery to insert her peritoneal dialysis catheter, when she was weak and scared, she'd insisted we stop at a stamp shop in Oakland, promising to be quick. At first I'd waited outside in the sun, but after a while, bored, I wandered in, just in time to watch the guy behind the counter add up her purchases, punching the price for each stamp on a little calculator: $6.00, $19.50, $11.00, $8.00, $14.00 . . . I watched as the total rose past a hundred dollars and—I couldn't help it— began to hiss at her in Spanish, *"How much are you going to spend?"*

"Just wait outside," she told me. But by that time I was transfixed; I watched as the total hit two hundred dollars, still climbing.

"Go outside, you'll just get upset."

"No." But finally I did, after the numbers hit three hundred and kept going up. I started the car, backed out of the parking space, waited in the street gunning the motor, wanting to just drive away.

Ana goes through wild swoops with her money—fierce budgeting followed by great extravagance; it's part of her nature as much as her raucous sense of humor, the way she eats, the way she makes love. And one way she deals with anxiety is by spending money; she's certainly not unique in that, and there are far worse things than stamps to spend money on. ("Some people spend big bucks on cocaine, or on prostitutes," Alison offers as consolation.) Because Ana and I have different incomes, different financial values and habits, we've always kept our money separate, splitting our expenses down the middle. But when Ana goes through one of her strict-budget phases I end up paying for things we do together: dinners out, weekends away. Then my resentment surges when a week or two or three later she swings the other way, goes on a spending binge for any one of her numerous costly hobbies: the tropical fish tank, the video games, the stamps.

Ana grew up poor. Her parents lived on credit; everyone they knew did. No one ever dreamed of paying off their balances each month. And later, through all the years of worsening health, doing and having what she wanted at the moment seemed a lot more important than good credit, a savings account, a stack of paid-in-full bills. This makes sense to me; and yet, because our lives are so joined that our money can never be truly separate, the differences chafe.

So driving down Highway 80 in the heat I ask myself what it was I'd wanted, anyway? Did I want her not to have gone to Reno? No; she'd wanted to go for so long, I'd felt she deserved the trip. Was it really the money that bothered me? Of course not; it's that I feel neglected, disappointed that she still seems to have so little interest in me, in lovemaking. I get tired of feeling that I'm throwing myself at her, making seductive or wistful suggestions, putting her hands on my body and hoping she'll get the hint. I want to *feel* her wanting me again.

I know, of course, why Ana's desire went away; it always does in organ failure, the body jealously guarding its energy for the essential. But Julia had said that Ana looked better than she had in years; in Reno I saw her vibrant, bright with excitement and energy—yet none of it was for me. *I'm jealous of Ana's devotion to those slot machines and stamps,* I think. *I want my lover back.*

The first time Ana came to my house was on a Tuesday night, four days after we'd met and spent much of the weekend making love. I invited her for dinner and cooked something with ginger and eggplant, something I now know she doesn't like—but she ate it gamely. I remember moving through the kitchen of the little house I lived in then, feeling her eyes and her hands on me, even from across the room. It was as if I were high or underwater, each movement made self-conscious by the intensity of her gaze.

After dinner we sat on the living room couch and I put on the Gipsy Kings, music my friend Jean-Paul had introduced me to; he'd told me it made him want to dance and sing and eat and drink and make love all at the same time. Ana knew the words to all the songs and sang them to me that night, not casually singing along, as I did, but serenading me with their pulse, their romantic fever. And I felt frightened, aroused, delighted. Felt finally matched, met, in some deep part of myself.

The next day she sent a dozen roses to my office. A few weeks later, for my birthday, she sent a bouquet of balloons.

It was a few weeks more before she told me she was diabetic. Beforehand she'd let slip some hints—"I don't have anything to hide from you," she said once, "but there's something about me I haven't told you yet, something most of the people close to me know." Images of exotic secrets, a husband and kids stashed away somewhere, flickered through my mind.

Other times, she alluded to her expectation that her life wouldn't be a long one. "What's the deal?" I asked finally, sitting her down on my couch one Saturday afternoon.

"I have diabetes."

"That's all?" I almost laughed. "So you have to give yourself a shot every day?" I knew that much, not a lot more.

She nodded.

"So when have you been doing it, the nights you've stayed here?"

"Out in my car in the morning." She looked embarrassed.

And I looked up diabetes a day or two later in one of the medical books at the AIDS hotline. I don't remember much of what I read; the book mentioned all the usual complications—circulation, nerves, eyes, kidneys, heart—but they weren't real to me then. Ana was healthy enough to make love all night; from what I could see (and I couldn't see much) she was taking care of herself. I wasn't worried. Besides, I thought, our relationship wasn't even serious.

Later I learned that she'd been told sometime in the mid '80s, by a doctor at the huge HMO where she was a patient then, that her kidneys already showed signs of damage and would someday fail. If there was anything she could do to retard the damage, she wasn't told; or, if she was, she didn't remember. Instead she simply incorporated the idea of eventual kidney failure into her emotional mythology; it became part of the way she thought about her life. If she wasn't going to live long, she'd better live good.

She declared from the beginning that she would never go on dialysis. She'd never seen a dialysis machine, never talked to anyone who'd been on one, but her mind was made up: that was no life worth living. And she didn't know much about transplantation, didn't know it would be possible for her. So she decided that when her kidneys failed she'd withdraw all the money from her retirement account and go on a cruise, live her last days in style.

This plan was so quintessentially Ana that when she told me about it, sometime during our first year together, I didn't even question it. Much later, of course, I laughed at the idea, gently, bitterly; belatedly, she laughed too. What a romantic image we'd had of kidney failure, tragic but conveniently asymptomatic, a perfect foil on which to sail off into the sunset; and how very different the reality of it was.

"I miss you," I tell her now, softly, my hands still on the steering wheel; these are the first words either of us has spoken for at least half an hour. When I look over toward her, I see that she's been crying too.

THREE

Dorey, my support group buddy, offers me a gift of a free bodywork session. She barely has the energy to work these days, she says, but she really wants to do this for me. So I search her out at her studio, a charming little office tucked away in a catacomb of artists' workshops, all surrounding a brick courtyard and a funky garden. The decor is classic bohemian Berkeley: carved mismatched benches, Buddha statues, a wild tangle of flowers. Three large, peaceful dogs are sprawled out on the bricks.

Inside, Dorey shows me where to put my clothes, gives me a clean white sheet to drape around myself. She puts on some soft New Age music, then motions me up onto the massage table. As she kneads my neck, tells me to let the weight of it into her hands, we begin to talk. She and Gene have been married just two years, have known each other for three.

"That's a hell of a short history together, to be facing what you're facing now," I comment, as if Ana's and my extra year together makes some ineffable difference.

"Yes. Do you mind if I work around your scar?" And she pulls at the tissue there, which doesn't hurt but feels sensitive, thinner than the rest of my skin.

"Within a few months of our marriage he began to have problems with his sexual—" she hesitates, "functioning. He blamed it on our relationship, said we weren't 'emotionally intimate' enough. I was relieved when I finally found out what the problem really was.

"It's funny," she says, "I remember telling him then that I'd still love him even if he couldn't—" she hesitates again, "function, sexually. And now that's what the deal is. I had no idea when we got married." Clearly this is an important point for her. *"No idea."*

"Would it have made a difference?" I ask.

"I really don't know." She's obviously troubled. And then, softly, "I would not have chosen willingly to walk into the situation I'm now in. Did *you* know?" she asks me then.

"At the time that I really made the commitment to Ana, I *did* know," I acknowledge. "I didn't know exactly what would happen, or when, but I knew she had major health problems. I knew," I add, echoing her words, "that that was part of the deal."

But Dorey and Gene's situation is so different from ours. In addition to the anguish of worrying about whether Gene will even live long enough to get transplanted, Dorey and Gene face financial crisis, too; both self-employed, they've got no sick time, no paid vacations, no organizational structure to provide support. Gene has health insurance, but it's a traditional indemnity plan that pays only 80 percent of his medical expenses. Transplantation is expensive; even the remaining 20 percent could add up to hundreds of thousands of dollars—which doesn't include the tens of thousands of dollars worth of medications he'd need to take afterward. And he doesn't qualify for state disability because, due to his time in graduate school, he worked one quarter too few in the last five years.

Financially Ana and I are blessed. Her health plan, an HMO, covers all her surgery and follow-up costs; her co-payment for each prescription is just seven dollars. So that's what she pays, now, for a ninety-day supply of Cyclosporine—actual cost $15,000. Yes, blessed. And her employer has a program that allows other employees to donate their vacation and sick-time hours to her; her co-workers have given her hundreds of hours already. After four months out of work she's still on full salary, between those donated hours and her disability pay.

"Liver failure makes people angry," Dorey says now. "It's part of the physiological response. The body realizes how endangered it is." And, she adds, Gene's been taking that anger out on her. "A few weeks ago I was thinking, 'I'll see him through the transplant, then leave,'" she tells me. "But it's been better since he realized on that last doctor's visit that he's dying."

The problem is that the doctors had initially projected doing Gene's transplant this month; when they saw how bad his liver enzymes were in February they thought they'd have to. But with his herbs and vitamins, blooming good health and denial, he's doing better than they'd expected, and the reward for that is more waiting; now they're saying they may not have to transplant him till next March, nine months from now.

"It's as if he's being punished for doing well."

"And he's *not* doing well," says Dorey grimly. "The other day we walked ten blocks and I thought he was going to keel over. Ten blocks!" she repeats, her voice incredulous.

I understand what she means, yet it makes me sad. It's been years since I could imagine Ana even attempting to walk that far.

When I get home Ana has bad news from her podiatrist. The foot ulcer she's had for six months now, a minor little sore on the sole of her foot, which started from a blister and never quite closed, is worse. She's been sloppy since she left the hospital, standing, walking on it more—who wouldn't be, given back the energy they'd lacked for so long? But a foot ulcer in a diabetic is a dangerous thing, and the immunosuppressive drugs she's on make it even more so. If the infection spread to the bone they'd have to amputate her foot; otherwise it could kill her.

So now she'll have to be on crutches, in a wheelchair, anything to keep the weight off that foot.

"And I'm *sick* of this," she spits out. "Sick of it!" And she's also terrified.

So there's no point in comparing our hardships with anyone else's; more to the point, there's no way to compare them.

I call Julia's house, leave another message on the machine. Still no word from her about Steve.

⊲⊗⊳

A rare summer heat wave has struck, and I wilt, as always, like a shade-loving plant. Oh, I love the sun; give me a nice seventy-five degree day, spiced up by a little breeze, and I'll luxuriate out on the deck like a lizard. But temperatures in the nineties immobilize me; I slump through the house, my contact lenses fogged; it's all I can do to prepare food and eat and clean up and run a few ice cubes along my skin, and then it seems it's time to start the whole cycle again. All through the long, rainy winter, days like this one were impossible to imagine; now I long for the cold, even for rain, anything to move my brain out of its heat-induced sludge so I can think and write and get things done again.

And Ana and I have been fighting, which we so rarely do—little, inconsequential spats that cause us both great pain, we're so raw already.

Thursday afternoon, after my session with Dorey, I was expecting some free hours, time to write and stretch and ponder, unhurried. But the house was chaotic, the dogs were hyperactive, and Ana was depressed and scared. I listened to her, stroked her hair. She wanted spaghetti, and I made it for her, cooking without a recipe, as I always do—but not creatively, for the pleasure of it, or even because I craved the food I was cooking. I'd cleaned the kitchen and done all the dishes that morning, but now it was dirty again, the sink suddenly, mysteriously piled high. Since Ana couldn't be on her feet, I'd have to wash them all. And I knew I needed to clean out the refrigerator, throw out the rotting leftovers to make room for the spaghetti. I opened the big white door, scanned the shelves, and felt utterly daunted.

I often feel this way, faced by household tasks. I envy the thoughtless, cheery efficiency I imagine other people mustering in these situations; I am, by nature, dreamy and lazy. I don't clean because I want to, only because I know that if I don't the mess will eventually make me feel even worse. It occurs to me again, as it has many times, what an utterly inappropriate temperament I have for the life I'm living at the moment; even the small tasks, and there are so many of them, wear at me so. I try to summon up some Zen consciousness, something about living in the moment, throwing myself fully into each thing I do, no matter how menial. If the aim is to make me feel better about it, it doesn't work. And yet, and yet, the refrigerator and dishes await. I do their bidding.

Then I watch an hour of TV with Ana, and then, at 11:00, after she limps to bed, I re-bandage her foot the way the podiatrist instructed (wash with Betadine, soak small piece of gauze in Betadine-water mixture and apply directly to ulcer, cover with larger piece of dry gauze, tape it all up). I bring her a glass of water, kiss her goodnight. "Feel you later," I say, as I always do, as she slowly turns the knob on the halogen lamp I bought her and the room fades dark.

It's 11:30. Now I finally have time to myself, the time I thought I'd have nine hours ago, and I'm too tired to use it. Tomorrow will be a day full of errands; I feel grumpy just thinking about it: a transplant clinic appointment, then a trip to look at wheelchairs for rent, then a fitting at the orthopedic shoe store, then dinner with one of Ana's friends, whom I like but am not close to—another day focused on Ana, not on me. *When will it be* my *turn?* I think—a dangerous thought.

❧

But the next morning traffic flows smoothly into the city. We sail down the highway in the sunshine, Ana dancing salsa in the passenger seat, and as we drive the Bay Bridge the whole city sparkles toward us. Even in our worst despair this drive could sometimes revive us. There was one Saturday when

Ana was still on hemodialysis, when the sun was bright and the Tex-Mex star Selena sang lustily out from the CD player, telling us we'd never find another love like hers, and with a particular poignance we knew that to be true—a berserk fan had murdered Selena just a few days earlier. Gorgeous sexy Selena, twenty-three years old, healthy and talented, a self-made millionaire, was dead; and we were alive, and the air bristled with clarity, the city skyline etched brightly against the roll of fog gathered high on the hill.

And today the clinic visit goes well; Ana is doing fine, the doctor assures us. The only big problem, apart from the foot, is her severe constipation; we learn now that it may be caused by the high dose of Procardia, the blood pressure medication, which is, in turn, necessitated by the Cyclosporine. Anti-hypertensive medications relax certain muscles; it seems her anal sphincter is one of them, too relaxed now to let her have a normal bowel movement. ("Your *culito's* on Qualuudes," I tease her later.) The doctors will try to figure something out, they say. Maybe she'll need to see a specialist. They'll work on it. But for now, every time she needs to defecate she'll have to put on a latex glove, squeeze on some lubricating jelly, and manually pull each turd out.

We have lunch at a Spanish tapas place in the Mission, flamenco guitar flowing through the speakers, rich food drenched in garlic and olive oil; we eat with abandon, sopping up the food's juices with our bread. In the restaurant bathroom I take off my shirt, splash cold water everywhere I can; back in the car we blast the air conditioner, invention of the gods.

It's at the therapeutic shoe store that we fight. I pull out an apple for dessert, and Ana says it'll "look funny" to her friend if I'm not hungry when we go out to eat, and suddenly I'm snarling that I didn't know my presence was required just for appearances. And then she's angry at me for speaking in English, making a scene that other people in the waiting room can understand, while she's been discreetly speaking Spanish. This is something cultural, I know; appearances in public places matter to her in a way they never have to me. I try to make up, but now Ana is in her clamming-up phase; I ask her in Spanish to talk to me, and she says she has nothing to say. I despise it when she withdraws like that, when I know she's holding back. "Bullshit!" I mouth at her in English, and then finally, in Spanish, we manage to sort of make amends.

But the next day we fight again.

We're rushing out of the house to get to a wheelchair store that closes in an hour. I didn't get the writing time I'd wanted in the morning. I stop to check the mail on our way out—it'll only take a minute, we've got plenty of time by my standards—and Ana asks, her voice heavy with annoyance, if I couldn't do that later, and I blow up, "Well, excuse me for forgetting that my only purpose in life is to be your chauffeur!"

It's an absurd thing to say, and it hurts her deeply.

Of course, these details aren't the point at all. The point is that I feel invisible, and I'm burned-out. Both of us were so ready for Ana to be better by now, and she *is* better, that's the irony; it's because she felt better that she overdid it with her foot, so she's back to living like an invalid again, and my life is again subsumed by caretaking, and both of us resent the hell out of it.

Finally, at night, we talk. We sit side by side, the way we sat when we went to counseling together for a few months last fall and winter, as Ana's kidneys failed. But now we're sitting on our bed instead of the counselor's sofa, facing the fan instead of Betsy's wry, mobile face. And after an hour or so of crying, taking turns listening to each other, we make our way partway through the hurt. We agree Ana will try to do more on her own; it'll be better for both of us that way. We'll try to separate out where she really *needs* my help, and where she doesn't. She's actually remarkably nimble in the rented wheelchair. We feel united again. We kiss.

And then we talk about sex.

With the fan's steady wind on our faces, with the hot evening's bright light fading to gray, we talk about sex: how scared she is that she'll never want it again, how that makes her tense up when I touch her or talk sexy to her, and how much it hurts me when she tenses up; it feels to me like a physical slap, makes me want to stop desiring her, and I do, for a few minutes, until the desire floats back up from the blow like water seeking its own level.

The other morning, for instance, she'd lain naked on our bed in the heat, her legs spread open to the fan, and I'd begun to admire her, first with my eyes, then with words, then with my lips. I bent to kiss her thick clump of hair, inhaled the scent of her, and told her in Spanish how I'd love to run my tongue slowly up this crevice, starting from down low and working forward, teasing her. It was always easier for me to sex-talk in Spanish, freed from the constraints of the language I grew up with, and with the words so much softer, more liquid than English.

And Ana began to hum, louder and louder, trying to drown out my voice.

And I withdrew, silenced, slapped.

"It's an involuntary reflex," she says now. "I get defensive, I get scared, I don't even realize what I'm doing. Tell me when I do that," she urges. "Stop me and ask me what I'm feeling."

But it's hard for me to do that when I feel so stunned and hurt myself.

I suggest we try one of those standard sex-therapy exercises, where I'll touch her everywhere but her genitals. No expectations, no disappointments; that's the idea, anyway. She agrees, thinks it might help take the pressure off.

And so the next morning when I wake up beside her, the sheet thrown half off our bodies in the heat, I begin to stroke her: her neck, which I love, its gentle slope into her ears, intricately whorled as shells, which I love; her forehead, warm and sweet and broad, now pebbled into acne by the Prednisone; her nose, her cheeks, her lips, the hollow of her throat, the rounded, heavy curves of her breasts—I try not to linger there, don't want to make her feel pressured—and the bumpy moonscapes of her nipples. I lean my body over hers, brushing her chest with my breasts; I kiss her belly, her groin, the long, not-quite-healed scar where they opened her up to put my kidney inside her. I stroke her thighs, her calves, her ankles and back up again to the thighs, careful to avoid the pubis; I stroke upward, loving her shoulders, her arms, the tender inner elbows, the large hands that have, so many times, reached into the center of me. I run my hands back up again to her breasts, her neck, and she lies still beneath my touch, not resisting it, not responding to it; and I *want* her to respond, want to feel excitement grow in her the way it grows in me with even the lightest touch of her skin against mine. I begin to touch her harder then, kneading her flesh, leaning over her again to lightly bite her neck, wanting to feel something from her, and—nothing.

"Is there some other way you'd like me to touch you?" I ask, desperately. "What feels good to you?"

"It all feels good," she says beatifically. "I'm just trying to relax, enjoy the sensations."

"You don't feel excited?"

"I'm not on that plane. I'm just relaxed."

And I realize that of course she's doing the exercise right and I, who'd suggested it, am doing it all wrong. I'm not supposed to be trying to excite her—waiting, hoping to excite her. I'm just supposed to be touching her—no goal, no agenda.

But touching her turns me on, and it makes no difference whether it's her *tota* or her hands, her breasts or shoulders or neck or belly; it's *her* I'm touching, and I want her. My nipples want her, and my mouth, and the electric pulse between my legs; and she knows it, feels it, and begins to pull at my nipples with both hands, nuzzling my ear with her lips at the same time; and so I give myself over to her the way I always do, placing my whole body and what feels, in this moment, like my entire life, into those hands of hers I love so well.

She maneuvers me onto my side, both of us on comfortable, familiar ground now, and keeps squeezing my nipples with one hand while the other hand moves down between my legs, stroking lightly, lightly, like a swimmer just barely breaking the surface in the warm thick pond I've become, until I push her fingers against me harder, writhing against her hand, angling her into me. She fixes her mouth on my ear again and I move against her, every cell in my body alive to her touch; my hands move on their own now, grabbing at the sheet, the pillow, the headboard; my teeth are clenched, my pelvis climbs toward her, up and up until I'm nothing but what she makes of me with her touch.

This is what there is between us, how she finds and answers me. How I give myself to her, my body, my life. And there was a time when the other half of this great dialogue was also spoken between us, when she handed me *her* body, *her* life, and I answered to the same deep fury in her flesh.

Always, when she takes me like this, I have the same thought. I tell it to her now: "I couldn't live without this."

And she says, "You don't have to."

Afterward, when she sits up, I curve myself around her back, unwilling to let go of the contact between our skin. "*No te suelto, jamás,*" I warn her. *I won't ever let you go.*

And she laughs and gently removes my hands and begins to perform her morning rites. She'll weigh herself to make sure she's not retaining fluid, take her temperature to make sure it's not elevated. She'll check her blood pressure with the arm cuff, prick her fingertip to test her sugar, then measure appropriate amount of two kinds of insulin—long- and short-acting—into a syringe, swab her belly with alcohol, and push the needle in. Then she'll shower, lower herself carefully down the stairs, and wheel herself around in her wheelchair in the kitchen, preparing breakfast.

⁂

Ana has always had very little body hair, skin smoother than any electrolysis could have made it; it's her Taino Indian ancestry. There's never even been any fuzz on her upper lip; I'm the one with the swarthy Mediterranean look. But now when I rub my cheek against her arm I feel a mass of tiny blonde hairs, and she's sprouted a thick new mustache. There are black hairs on her belly that weren't there before, and another blonde expanse on her back. Mornings, while she's still asleep, I watch her transformed body, fascinated, waiting to see where and how she'll change next. I don't mention it to her, but of course eventually she notices.

"I've got a mustache!" she glares at me one day.

"I know."

She examines her body with disgust. "Look at me, *to'a pelu'a*!"

"*Mi melocontonsota*," I croon. *My giant peach.*

Another morning she wakes up and stares from the mirror to the framed photo of Frida Kahlo hung by our bed, then back to the mirror again. "I look like Frida!" she pronounces. "Look how my eyebrows are growing together. I used to have little lines that went in an arc; now look at them."

"*Fridita, como te has engordado,*" I tease. *Frida, how plump you've gotten.* I kiss her eyebrows, her eyelids; I rub my lips against her furred cheeks. When we touch lips I feel her mustache hairs; I suck at her upper lip, tonguing them.

They call this hirsutism in the drug insert leaflets; it's a relatively common side effect of both Prednisone and Cyclosporine. And, in and of itself, it's not a big deal; it bothers me not at all, and though Ana complains, adjusting to this visibly new body, she's at least half joking. Still, it's another reminder of all those drugs working within her, altering her in ways we can't fully understand.

❧

It's my second day due back at work and I'm rushing around the kitchen like one of those Indian goddesses with eight arms, trying to get my lunch ready when I should be on my way out the door already, and Ana is bumping around the kitchen in her wheelchair trying to make her breakfast before she has to go to the lab for her weekly blood draw, and everywhere she is—in front of the refrigerator, blocking the counter, in awkward transit to the table—is a place I can't be. She doesn't have to leave till a half-hour later than I do, I think, so why is she getting in my way?

But what's hardest for me is how angry she is; I feel it in the way she slams the refrigerator door, shoves plates across the counter, clattering. I'm tired of her anger, I'm tired of her foot ulcer, I'm tired of her wheelchair in my way, and I'm late for work; and so, again, we fight.

"If you'd just tell me what you need I could bring it to the table for you," I say, trying to make my voice sound helpful, hearing it come out surly instead.

"I was trying to get everything myself. I know you don't have much time."

"Well it would take a lot *less* time for me to just get you what you need, instead of having to work around you, which takes ten times as long," I explode, and Ana crumples suddenly into shaking sobs, covering her face with her hands.

Instantly contrite, I go to try to hug her and she rears back up at me, "Don't touch me! Just don't touch me!"

And I can't leave the house now. I call work, tell them I'll be late.

A few minutes later Ana says, raising her face angrily, "I'm not mad at you; I'm mad at being in this stupid wheelchair! How do you think it feels to me, trying to live like this?"

"How do you think it feels to *me*, doing all the housework and taking care of someone who doesn't even touch me or look at me with any kind of desire?"

"How can I look at you with desire when I don't even feel like a human being?"

"What will it take to make you feel like a human being?" I challenge her.

"A feeling that I have some control over my life, that's what!"

"And when will *that* be? Right now the problem is your foot. Next it'll be something else. There's always going to be something."

"Maybe I should just leave," Ana says, as she always does when she feels desperate.

"Maybe you should just go to a counselor—that would be more to the point!" I'm glaring at her now.

"Oh yeah? What's a counselor going to do, 'validate my feelings'?" Ana sneers.

"Help you *deal* with your feelings. Your problem right now isn't just your foot, it's *here*." I tap one finger lightly against the side of her head.

"Are you saying my foot is in my head?" yells Ana, willfully obtuse.

And so on.

And we're both right, of course, as always; and we're both so stressed we can hardly hear each other. Loving is hard under these conditions. My own anger frightens me.

And the foot ulcer is healing so slowly—if it's healing at all. Every morning and every night I re-bandage the ulcer, cleaning it with a little Betadine, then packing it with a diluted Betadine poultice the way the podiatrist instructed. And some days I think it looks better—smaller, shallower. Other days I can't see any improvement at all. Maybe Ana should see a specialist in diabetic foot ulcers, I think. Maybe there's something else that can be done. With all the high-tech medical procedures and equipment and drugs around, surely there's some way to deal with a little hole on the sole of the foot—some way other than cutting the foot off or just waiting, waiting endlessly, for a badly damaged body to slowly heal itself?

❦

These are some things about Ana:

She's not only punctual, she actually likes to be early. If she's going to a training that starts at 8:00 and is a half-hour's drive away, she'll leave the house before 7:00; she enjoys being the first one there, getting her coffee, choosing her seat, watching everyone else arrive. I, on the other hand, will leave at 7:40, balancing a mug of tea on the dashboard as I drive, counting on the fact that the training won't start on time anyway (in part because they'll be waiting for latecomers like me).

Ana always gets gas when her gauge registers half full—any lower than that and she gets nervous. "Do we have enough gas to make it home?" she'll ask. I do the math for her: half of a twenty-gallon tank means ten gallons; her car gets at least twenty miles per gallon, which means we could go another two hundred miles, and home is less than twenty miles away. Completely unconvinced, Ana steers us toward the nearest station anyway. In my own car I drive until the red E light comes on, even past that point; I can go at least eighteen miles more after the light comes on, I've found, although of course I've run out of gas more than once finding that out.

Ana keeps her car immaculate; she gets it washed at the full-serve car wash every two weeks. My car is littered with banana peels and apple cores, the dashboard stained from a season's worth of beverages not balanced quite successfully enough; every few months I pick up the largest hunks of trash.

And Ana is ferociously obedient to the doctors' rules now, post-transplant. "Compliant," they call it. "I wish all my patients were like you," one doctor praised her, looking over her neatly written records: each day's weight, blood pressure, blood sugar, temp; every pill accounted for. When they tell her to take her Cyclosporine twelve hours before the morning blood draw, so they'll get a consistent reading of the levels it's reached in her blood, she times it down to the minute.

And now I learn what this compliance is costing her.

"I make myself into a robot," she tells me. "Every time I take my pills I shut my feelings off."

"What would happen if you didn't?"

"I wouldn't take them." Her eyes fill with tears. She rocks back and forth in the hallway in her wheelchair, crying silently.

Ana has been diabetic since she was sixteen. She grew up watching her mother, also diabetic, being rushed to the hospital, comatose from high blood sugar—not once, but many times. Home blood sugar testing didn't even exist then; urine could be tested, but the tests weren't terribly accurate, and most of the time her mother didn't bother anyway. It seemed so useless; the doctors told her not to eat rice, pasta, bread, and that was what she fed her family—that was what they wanted to eat, what all Puerto Ricans ate, and it was also all they could afford. "She'd make a big pot of *arroz y habichuelas*, rice and beans, for all of us and just sit there watching us eat, trying to soothe her hunger with a cup of coffee," Ana recalls. "She'd serve herself one little bowlful. She tried to hold back. And she'd do that for a while but then she'd break down, eat some *pastelillos de guayaba* or one of the other sweets she loved. There wasn't any Nutrasweet back then.

"We didn't have a car, so when she started feeling dizzy, with a certain kind of headache, we'd just call a cab. All of us girls and her and my dad would pile in. Sometimes she'd pass out before we got to the hospital. The year before she died she was in a coma for two weeks. It was a miracle God returned her to us that time.

"If she had lived she'd have been blind by now, in a wheelchair. Probably her kidneys would have failed, too. Everything I'm going through now—hah, my mother couldn't have done it. She was *muy vanidosa*, very vain. *Es mejor que pasó como pasó*." *It's better that things happened as they did.*

Ana wasn't really the youngest in her family, just the last child who lived. After her there were two early stillbirths, one a boy who would have weighed twenty pounds. Ana herself weighed fourteen pounds at birth; since pregnancy wreaks havoc on blood sugar, diabetics' babies are notorious for high birth weight. Even as a young child, Ana says, she knew she too would be diabetic; *era el destino*, it was fated that her mother's suffering would be hers as well.

At fifteen, the year before her diabetes diagnosis, Ana realized that she was a lesbian. She'd been fantasizing about women for years; suddenly, an offhand comment by a friend made her understand what that meant. So when, at sixteen, the diagnosis came and she knew she was doomed not once but twice, she wrote a long, passionate, explicit love letter to one of her female teachers.

The shocked teacher showed the letter to the school principal, and the school administrators held a hurried conference. Either Ana would see the school psychiatrist, they decided, or they would tell her parents. She chose the psychiatrist, whom she saw twice a week for nearly three years, and whose main therapeutic strategy was to encourage her to have sex with men. Desperate and alone, Ana tried to kill herself with sleeping pills he'd prescribed. Somehow it backfired, and she went sleepless for three days instead. She was the youngest of five children, all preoccupied with their own lives; her mother was ill, her father withdrawn; no one even noticed.

Since her life hadn't ended, it continued. The only good thing that came of her sessions with the psychiatrist was that he told her she was smart. She was "college material," he insisted. She was dumbfounded at first; her grades were lousy, she spent her class time daydreaming. No one in her family had ever attended college. But week after week the psychiatrist repeated himself, and she began to study more, found she could master the material; in one semester she went from a D average to straight As. She graduated from high school with honors, bid the psychiatrist (who believed by that time that he had cured her) goodbye, and registered at the University of Puerto Rico.

She ignored her diabetes as much as possible then; she took pills, that was all. She didn't worry about whether her blood sugar was well-controlled; at least she didn't go into comas like her mother. She worked, went to school, thought about women, fought with her father and brother. When she was nineteen her mother died, and Ana stood proud in her isolation and grief; she wore red to her mother's funeral, and the rest of the family fumed. Her sisters were married already; they couldn't understand the world she lived in. Her oldest brother, suspecting her lesbianism, ordered her out of the house, and she lived with friends for the last few months of her senior year in college.

She was formulating her plan. She'd never even kissed a woman, but she knew what she was, what she wanted. She majored in psychology, read all the then-prevalent theories about homosexuality: nature or nurture, sickness or perversion or "alternative lifestyle." The year she'd started college, 1973, was also the year the American Psychiatric Association removed homosexuality from its list of mental illnesses; they replaced it with "homosexual dysphoria," labeling as mentally ill only those homosexuals who were unhappy with their sexual orientation. That didn't prevent some of Ana's professors from raving about *los maricones*, but there was one who was more liberal, who specialized in sexuality; Ana spent hours reading and underlining each chapter he assigned, stayed after class to talk to him. "I have a friend who thinks she may be a homosexual," she told him finally.

"Your friend should go to San Francisco. She can have a better life there," he said kindly. He'd just come back from a trip to California the year before. "Gay people can live more openly there. There's nothing for her here."

And so a few months later, with her college diploma, a set of suitcases her grandmother had given her, five hundred dollars, and a guitar, Ana went. Slowly she found friends, a job, the gay bars. She even got good health care for a while, through a city-run program. The fees were low and she paid them promptly, but after a year or so the billing department messed up, insisting she owed them money. They cut off her services, and she never fought, never went back. It was years before she saw a doctor again.

When she did, the doctor told her she needed to begin injecting herself with insulin. "I felt I'd sunk to the lowest point I could sink to," she tells me now. "I felt like a junkie, a drug addict. I felt unclean. I couldn't do it, but I couldn't live if I didn't."

"How did you get beyond those feelings?" I ask, and she shrugs.

"But you did get past them? You don't feel that way now?"

"I do it because I know I have to," she says.

And now there is so much more she has to do, my proud rebel who survived by ignoring her own health for so many years; and she does it—does it expertly—but she rages inside.

We talk about sex again, and her despair comes flooding out. "Do you know what it's like to have to stick your finger up your butt every single time you need to take a crap? *No te puedes imaginar.* It's humiliating. It makes me bleed. It hurts. My body's not working right. How can I want you to touch me?"

She'd seemed so good-natured about the problem, adapted so well, carrying the lubricant and latex gloves around with her; we'd even joked about it. I'd had no idea it was affecting her this way.

"Call the transplant clinic. Right now," I tell her.

And the doctor on duty prescribes yet another blood pressure medication, and she tries it, as ordered, along with one Procardia instead of two. Not much improvement, though her blood pressure falls below normal.

"My suggestion would be," I say carefully, the next day, "to try stopping the Procardia. The new drug may control your pressure on its own. At least that way we can find out if the Procardia is the problem."

"I don't know if I should," Ana says worriedly.

"Call the clinic and ask the doctor, then."

But her blood pressure is fine, so that evening she takes my suggestion, swallows only the new pill. Within an hour she has her first normal bowel movement in over a month.

"My only regret," I say later, both of us jubilant, "is that we didn't insist harder, sooner, that something be done about this."

And later still, reflecting, I say to no one in particular, "But why didn't they change your blood pressure medication sooner? When one Procardia a day wasn't enough, why did they quadruple the dose of that one, rather than trying something else? There are a million blood pressure medications on the market. Did Procardia have the biggest ad this month in the nephrologists' journal, or what?"

"Maybe," Ana shrugs.

"You know, the drug companies do run big ads in all the medical journals," I muse. "But you want to believe that that doesn't influence the doctors; you know, that's what makes regular people want Pepsi instead of Coke, or whatever, but you don't want to believe that your doctors are prescribing meds for you based on which company has the cleverest copywriter, or the biggest advertising budget."

And yet I suspect that may be exactly what happens. But maybe, I hope, I just don't know enough.

⌘

Ana spends her days in the wheelchair now; she's really been staying off her foot this time, yet the ulcer still doesn't seem to be improving. Okay, says Ana, she'll ask the podiatrist about seeing a specialist. But it's Thursday now; she's got an appointment for next Tuesday, doesn't want to deal with it till then. I picked up a freebie magazine at the health food store the last time we went shopping; now I see it mentions aloe vera, says it's good for wounds. We have an aloe plant right in the kitchen. That night at bandage-changing time I cut off a piece of leaf and squeeze some of its greenish-yellow sap onto the ulcer.

By morning the aloe has stained Ana's skin a surprising dark purple, but the ulcer looks smaller, I think. I want to believe. For the next five days I faithfully use aloe twice a day instead of Betadine. Each time I cut off another bit of leaf I say a silent little grateful prayer to the plant, which I've now moved to the bathroom. And now I can finally *see* the ulcer getting better; each morning, each night, there's more change. It's closing up.

On Tuesday the podiatrist confirms that the ulcer is much improved. "Whatever you're doing, keep doing it," he tells Ana. Another two weeks and it'll be closed, he says.

To me this sounds like wonderful news, yet Ana is despondent. She hears the podiatrist's words as a sentence: another two weeks in jail, the jail that wheelchair is to her.

She's despondent; I'm angry. Her despondence makes me angry; my anger makes *me* despondent. We're trapped in a cycle where any small thing can set either of us off. *Una gota más en un cuarto lleno de agua* is Ana's description for this state. *One more drop in a room already filled with water.* "The straw that broke the camel's back?" I suggest, translating to an idiom I'm familiar with, and she agrees.

One morning she says, "I think when I go back to work I'll go full time. My job isn't physically strenuous; I think I can handle it."

And I instantly rage inside, *Sure you think you can handle it—because you're so used to having me as your cook and maid!* I grit my teeth and say calmly instead, "When you think about your energy, please keep in mind that I don't want to keep doing all the housework forever. Please factor that in." My faked calm sounds icy, and some tears bubble up halfway through my sentence. Ana doesn't respond. I drive to work fuming, *I won't do it! I won't!*

In December and January, when Ana's kidneys were failing fast, I had urged her over and over to cut her hours at work, go down to part time. "I'm not ready," she insisted. So I began getting up with her at five every morning; her body ache was so severe I had to soap her up and rinse her in the shower. As her energy lessened, she had to begin showering at night; if she tried to do it in the morning she'd be too exhausted to dress, even with my help. Downstairs I made her breakfast, packed a lunch for her; then she half-limped, half-staggered to the car. Driving itself wasn't too hard, but it took her fifteen minutes just to walk across the street from the parking lot to the elevator, then down the hall to her office. Every morning when she got there she'd collapse behind her shut door and nap a while. There were weeks of this, weeks while she clung to working full time. Then in February, ostensibly because of the foot ulcer, she decided to stop working for two weeks, and after that she never went back.

Oh yes, Ana's work ethic is noble, her will is astounding, *but*. But *I* don't intend to go through that again. If she doesn't have the energy to work full time *and* do at least 50 percent of the housework *and* have some energy left over for me, she'll have to work part time. I won't stand for anything less. My head is filled with a buzzing fury; I can hardly concentrate at work. *I won't do it, I won't do it,* I'm chanting inside.

I don't know what to do with so much anger.

Weeks later a therapist whom we've heard of through our transplant support group, a woman who had a liver transplant herself several years ago, sends me an article titled, "In Sickness and in Health: The Impact of Illness on Couples' Relationships." I cry as I read,

> "Couples need to be forewarned that having intense and seemingly irrational emotions is natural in situations of illness and disability . . . Especially in young couples, the well partner often feels both resentful about constricted life cycle options, and shame about such feelings . . . The sense of loss and being robbed is acute."

The article suggests that therapists work with couples to "normalize" feelings such as "intense anger, ambivalence, death wishes, escape fantasies . . . to counteract secrecy, shame and well partner/survivor guilt."

It helps only a little to realize we're a textbook case.

Mornings, we wake perfect.

I curve my belly around her ass, my chest presses against her back, the soft new hairs on her neck whisper to my lips.

Or: she turns onto her other side, my lips burrow between her breasts, my breastbone nestles comfortably against her rib, and I feel wholly soothed.

Or: her head rests near my collarbone, and I inhale her hair like a meadow. Her cheek is on my breast, and my entire body curves to echo its touch. Our legs are knit together, our bellies mashed into a single shape.

It isn't always this way. Sometimes one or both of us doesn't sleep well and we wake grumpy, dissatisfied. Sometimes the dogs wake us with their barking and I feel myself tense up with frustration; one of us, and that means me, has to get out of bed and tromp downstairs and try to quiet them. This morning, in fact, the cats began playing with something under the bed around 5:30 A.M., and then the dog who sleeps in our room woke up and began scratching—the fleas have been particularly ferocious this year, after all the winter rains—and the metal tags on her collar jangled together like a tambourine. There's a very particular fury I feel when I want, *need*, more sleep, and can't get it. That fury, tense and cold in my chest, made it harder for me to go back to sleep.

But finally we slept again, Ana and the cats and the dog and I, and I dreamed Ana and I were fighting horribly. In the dream she had to soak her foot in hot water; wanting to spare me the work, she carried the water into the bedroom herself, limping awkwardly, the water sloshing out from the basin. And she'd used a basin that had had kitty litter in it: dirty litter still clung to the sides; it stank. How could she soak her foot in that? I was furious at her for the effort she'd made and for not doing it *right*, and I yelled at her and seized the basin and scrubbed and scrubbed until it was really clean, filled it with more water, brought it back to her. But by that time she no longer wanted to soak her foot. She lay on the bed with her body and face turned away from me, and my fury rose higher—I wanted some response from her and she would give me none—and so I poured the water on her body where she lay.

That was only part of the dream. There was more, all infused with the same wild desperate anger that built and built and built on itself until it felt to me like it would destroy us both.

We wake and I tell her about the dream. We press together and I feel renewed. Our bodies have always conversed so fluently with each other; they discovered our love first and we followed them, flailing and stumbling, into it, and they guide us still. Just last night I felt so weary and hope-less, so hurt by Ana's lack of physical desire, so disappointed and burdened by her depression, that I wondered whether my passion for her could sur-vive. And this morning the answer comes to me again, as it has so many other mornings—not as a thought, an idea, but as a presence. This passion between us isn't mine to control or fear, to grasp or lose. It doesn't come *from* me, but rather *through* me; it comes from the world.

And on a more pragmatic level I think—because my brain keeps ticking away alongside, in spite of, these moments of revelation—that as long as Ana and I keep talking, as long as we can let this anger out, it doesn't have to destroy us. I've never seen therapy as a panacea, I've known plenty of peo-ple apparently unhelped by years and years of it, but these days I feel like a broken record; counseling, I keep saying, we need help, you need help, I need help, we need help. I wish Ana would see a counselor on her own; cou-ples counseling can work on the ways this crisis plays itself out between us, but I know there's much more she's dealing with on her own. And yet she's resolute. A counselor wouldn't help, she says. The circumstances are the problem. When she can walk again . . . When she can go back to work . . . When she can lead a more normal life again . . . she'll feel better.

And, briefly, she convinces me.

But then I remember how when she was on hemodialysis—the two fat catheter lines jutting from her neck, their needles poking at her whenever she moved her head—we said to each other: peritoneal dialysis will be so much better. After all, the doctors said she'd be able to do that at home, at night, while she slept. And then when she was on peritoneal dialysis, she despised the tube coming from her belly, the machine she had to thread it into every night, the hours of having her body filled with fluid and then drained, filled and then drained, and the times when the electronic con-trol panel would register some error and BEEPBEEPBEEPBEEP us awake, the frantic 2:00 A.M. phone calls to the 24-hour service line to try to figure out what was wrong. So things were not better, but worse.

And then again we waited for it to be better after the transplant; and here we are ten weeks later, her new kidney working fine, both of us healed from surgery, yet things are worse again. And so when I hear her say, "After my foot heals . . . After I go back to work . . . " I want to hope, want to believe, but I am terrified too that those changes will bring their own problems, that we will never be done with waiting for circumstances to change.

Ana wheels herself awkwardly back and forth through the hall and says, "All these doctors' appointments, I've had it up to here with them. It's exhausting; I'm sick of going to the doctor, and still I've got to go to the gynecologist to get my hormones checked, and I have to call the eye doctor to get the cataract surgery, and I go back to the transplant clinic next week, and I get my blood drawn twice a week, and how'm I supposed to *live* if all I do is go to the doctor?"

And she says, "And all these medications, you know they've got to be affecting me. I *know* my body. All these pills I'm taking every day, they must have some impact on my moods."

And my eyes fill with tears when I listen to her, when I manage to really hear *her* voice and not just my own ready with answers, suggestions, retorts, frustration—because of course she is right: the managing of this transplant and her diabetes and all its complications, the managing of her survival in this physical body, is an enormous task.

But these are things that will not change.

And so this is what I always come back to: that somehow, and I don't claim to know how, we have to change ourselves.

⬿

Now Ana begins to have weak spells, times when she feels suddenly dizzy, all the energy drained out of her. "Must be the medications," she says wearily. "Maybe it's the Imuran." Of all her pills, the Imuran is her favorite culprit, ever since that night when she had the nightmares.

I have a different theory. "Maybe your blood pressure is going too *low*, now. Let's test it the next time you feel that way." Sure enough, her pressure is 100 over 60.

"Maybe you don't need as much blood pressure medication now," I say, hopefully. "It's over-correcting you."

Ana is dubious. "I'll bring it up with the doctors, next time I go in."

The weakness continues.

At her next clinic visit the doctor says, "Sure, stop the new medication. Remember, you're still on the other antihypertensive, plus the diuretic, plus the angina drug."

So the new drug we fought so hard for, the one tiny little pill that had proved an effective replacement for the four big Procardia tablets—too effective a replacement, in fact—is now out. We re-do Ana's pill box again.

The following week the podiatrist pronounces Ana's foot ulcer cured.

"It was the aloe that did it," Ana tells him. "All those months and months when we used Betadine it didn't close. The aloe vera healed it in just a few weeks."

The doctor laughs indulgently, dismissively. "Oh, aloe's been used for centuries," he says. "Maybe I should recommend that to *all* my patients." Of course, we know he's only joking.

⁂

It's a bright, sunny, windy evening, the moon large and pale in the still-blue sky. It seems like a long time since we sat here in the hot tub in the backyard, naked together in the warm water, the wind keeping us just chilled enough. From my favorite corner, the jets running hot on the small of my back, I look over at Ana: her ruddy face, strong arms, deliciously fat breasts lying low on her chest. The water comes up to her breastbone, so I can't see the scars on her belly; from where I sit she looks perfectly healthy, as if none of the past year had happened. And looking at this upper portion of her body, apparently intact, somehow I see instead how much she has been altered, how much she's lost, and how much pain and grief and rage are with her still. Compassion stings at my eyes; my anger drains from me as I look at her, really *see* her; and, perhaps because for once I am not distracted by the physical scars she bears, I see also how her spirit has been scarred, and how slow it will be to recover.

"It will take a long time for you to heal," I say, and although no words of this kind have passed between us before, she understands me in mid-thought and answers simply, "Yes."

"I miss the person you used to be," I tell her in Spanish.

"What was that person like?" It's as if she's asking me for a bedtime story.

"*Más alegre,* more joyous. With more energy, passion, not just sexually but passion *por la vida.*"

"Yes," she agrees sadly, and in the water I cross over to her and we touch, our flesh released of weight.

It's not simple, I think, no matter how much we want it to be. There's that idea that when you survive a crisis, forever afterward your priorities are in order, you're so grateful for each precious moment, and so on. Well, there *is* that, of course, but there isn't *only* that. This other feeling is real too, the other side of trauma's aftermath: this fumbling around in the rubble our lives have become. We will rebuild, we will be happy again; in fact, we are already happy, even as we are sad. But the rebuilding is slow, all the old plans have been lost; we mourn even as we carry bricks.

FOUR

There are just three of us in attendance at the first meeting of the caregivers' support group that Dorey and I have organized in my living room: Dorey and me, of course, and also Erich, whose wife, Sarah, is waiting for a liver.

Dorey is thirty-eight, an activist, poised, lovely, and articulate. She cries easily, then forces herself back to composure. She wields clippings from medical journals, book lists, printouts from the Internet.

Erich is fifty, a huge bearded frog-like man stuffed into a button-down shirt and tie; he's a mid-level manager with one of the major banks. He speaks with a southern drawl; his voice sounds calm, even jovial, no matter what he's saying. We won't see any tears from *him*.

And I, tonight, am tired. Ana and I have talked and fought and talked so much these past weeks, I have nothing left to pour out; and I feel badly, too, because I'm on the other side of the divide from Dorey and Erich. Ana is post-transplant, alive and well; Gene and Sarah grow sicker each day, their prognoses are uncertain. How can we support each other?

Dorey tells us several stories.

"I was doing bodywork on a woman I know, a psychologist, last week. She was grieving for her friend, who had just died very suddenly of meningitis. And I found myself asking her, 'What was her blood type? Was she in good health?' Like a vulture," she says ruefully, and we laugh.

The second story is one Dorey heard secondhand.

"This woman was waiting for a liver transplant, getting sicker and sicker. Finally she decided to go to the hospital, but she really wasn't well enough to drive. On her way there she hit a teenage girl; they were both brought to the same emergency room. The girl died, and the woman was given her liver."

We're stunned into silence.

"It's destiny," Dorey says. "Whatever happens, it's destiny."

Gene is a little better this week, she tells us. He's got more energy; even his numbers have improved a little. It's thrown him back into denial. He's back to saying he's going to heal himself. It drives Dorey crazy, yet she knows that denial is part of what may help Gene survive.

Sarah is down to ninety-six pounds. "She doesn't even like to leave the house anymore," Erich says. "She says she smells bad."

"Liver disease does have a very specific smell," Dorey agrees. "It's the bile, coming out through the pores."

And Sarah is in constant pain. She has a T-tube, a surgically implanted device that helps channel bile around her gallbladder, and it's always infected. It's getting hard for her to breathe. Her legs are so diseased that the slightest pressure makes them swell up like balloons. Erich reports all this to us with his casual inflection unchanged.

"And how are *you* coping?" we ask.

"Two Prozacs a day. And I listen to meditation tapes on my commute. I'm into Indian visions.

"I was born with a bad heart," Erich tells us suddenly. "They told me I wouldn't live past thirty. Before I got married, settled down, I used to ride a Harley. If the wife dies, maybe I'll go back to that. Sell everything, hit the road."

When they turn to me I talk about how depressed Ana's been. How it seems like it should be enough for both of us, just having her alive—and yet it isn't. "I feel like we're supposed to be appreciating each moment, stopping to smell the roses and all that. But it isn't that easy."

And so the conversation shifts to roses. We actually do have a bunch of rose bushes in the backyard; we planted them in April, the month before the surgery. Down in Union City, where I work, a huge flower growing company had been sold to a housing developer; dozens of greenhouses were being torn down, thousands of rosebushes were being plowed into the ground. I was so bruised and fragile and exhausted then, and the roses were such a wonder—huge old plants grown almost into trees, covered with plate-sized blooms—that it seemed like a holocaust to me. So Ana and I and a bold friend drove down there one Sunday, when the demolition crews weren't there, and dug up about twenty of them. Some died of shock, but most survived; even some we'd thought were gone are coming back now, sprouting shiny new red leaves from their graying wood stalks.

Dorey's eyes glow. "I wish I'd known. We *love* roses. We have a bunch of them in pots. Actually, Gene's just started noticing them more; this past week when he's had more energy, he's even been watering them."

"When we moved up here from Southern California we brought some of our roses with us," Erich says. "There were already some roses at our new house; we planted the old ones right next to them. It looked like they weren't going to make it at first, but now they've taken off; they're enormous, even bigger than the others." He beams.

It's a great comfort, talking about roses.

⌗

It's August 11, our three-month transplant anniversary.

Today Ana went by her office in preparation for her return to work. Walking down the long marble hall she remembered just how bad she felt last February, before she went out on disability—how it exhausted her to navigate the building, how she had to sit and rest on every bench she passed. Now she parked a block away. "I was only a little out of breath when I got there," she reports proudly. And all her co-workers told her how good she looks, and it's true—"*Como si nada,*" Ana says. *As if nothing had happened.*

"Does it seem to you like a miracle?" I ask. We're lying on our bed together, naked in the heat, the ceiling fan whirring sweetly down on us. I hear that word so often—*miracle*—and it makes me uneasy. It sounds too simple, as if Ana's new life had been that easily bestowed.

But Ana nods yes: it *is* a miracle. An organ I was born with, an organ that grew and functioned in my body for thirty-three years, now works in her body instead. And physically I feel no different; and physically Ana's existence has been transformed.

I finger her scar, the fat, angry-looking gash, closed-over now, finally, with the help of some more leaves from the aloe plant, and the little row of red-dot welts above and below it, left by the staples the surgeons closed her with. I finger my own scar, the thin, five-inch pink line neatly angled down my right side. Whenever people ask about the transplant I pull my shirt up to show it to them, friends and strangers and co-workers, at work, at the supermarket; I show it to them as if otherwise they won't believe me—and yet it feels to me like *I'm* the one who does not, will never, comprehend.

And maybe it's because she feels stronger now, because she's finally heading back to work, that Ana agrees to return to counseling with me, as well.

One day at work I look something up in the *Physician's Desk Reference* and my gaze lands on the next entry in the book: OKT3. Guiltily, fearfully, I mark the page, finish my other tasks as quickly as I can, hunch over the book again. In a way it's funny I didn't think of looking the drug up earlier, here at work with all these medical books at hand. But it's not as if we had any choice about Ana taking it, not like we could have read about it, considered, given an informed yes or no; and so I never looked.

I look now.

The stats are worse than I'd thought, worse than I'd seen before. I flip the book closed, check the cover date; no, it's current. Well, these stats don't really apply to Ana because they're for people who've received cadaver transplants, I remind myself; the results are always better with living donors. Still: 80 percent *patient* survival after one year. Seventy percent after two years. That's not even talking about the kidney; that's talking about the *people*.

"Love," my friend Alison says when I talk to her later. "Remember, love changes the odds too. Ana has so much love in her life."

Once I didn't believe in things like that. Now I do. That's my problem; I believe everything I read. And I read it all with equal avidity, the medical journals and the PDR and the junk mail I get with its envelopes screaming *Cure yourself with fruits and vegetables! What the medical establishment doesn't want you to know!* I believe the studies I've read about prayer, how even the people who didn't know they were being prayed for did better than those who weren't prayed for at all; and I believe the studies showing that love, a loving partner and community of friends, are as significant a determinant of longevity as blood pressure or cholesterol or anything else the doctors can quantify; and I believe the statistics, right here in front of me in black and white—only I don't know where among those numbers the woman I love will fall.

One night in a counseling session Ana brought up her old plan of going on a cruise when her kidneys failed. "You weren't counting on being in love, having a life you liked well enough to want to stick around," Betsy observed matter-of-factly, and Ana nodded in confirmation; and that comes back to me now, Betsy's comment, Ana's nod. How entwined with each other we have become, that I have given Ana both a reason to go on living and the means to do so.

"I'm like my Titi Nina Fe," Ana says, "*bien pegada a la vida.*" It's one of the Spanish expressions I love best, not easily translatable. "Very attached to life" conveys part of it; but the verb *pegar* means *to glue*, so I hear Ana saying more literally that she is well-glued to life, she won't be easily pried loose.

Another of her phrases is *nadie te puede quitar lo bailado. No one can take away what you already danced.* There's no real English equivalent for that one either: maybe "It's no use crying over spilt milk," but that doesn't translate the sense of celebration; you didn't just spill your milk, you didn't just screw up your life—you *danced* it, too. That's what Ana says when we talk about all the years she didn't take care of herself, when I speculate about what might have happened differently, *if only, if only.* If I'd known more about diabetes when we got together, influenced her to start monitoring her blood sugar then, four years earlier. If her nephrologist had told us the truth about the low-protein diet when I asked him about it, a year before her kidneys failed. If she'd gotten better education from her doctors back in the '80s, when blood tests first picked up the decline in her kidney function; if they'd told her then that there were things she could do.

Ana just shrugs at this line of thinking. "*Nadie me puede quitar lo bailado.*" And I think of a time when she actually danced, when we'd been dating only a few months and she put on a salsa tape and shimmied naked before me. I watched her, torn then between my desire for her and the part of me that saw her as unbeautiful, fat and ungainly; and yet her body took the music's rhythm in, radiated with it, *became* it, until the movement in her shoulders, chest, belly, and hips was irresistible to me, and I grabbed at her, wanting her, and she spun toward the other side of the room, laughing, feeling her power. *No one can take away what we've already danced.*

I finish the PDR entry: *Long-term effects of* OKT3 *unknown* (you're lucky if you live long enough to get to worry about the long term, I guess). And there's the obligatory paragraph about *lymphoproliferative diseases, including lymphoma.* All the post-transplant meds increase the risk of those diseases; it's not known, the book says, just how much that risk is augmented by the addition of OKT3. But then this:

> Lymphoma in transplant recipients, when it does occur, is generally diagnosed soon after transplant, usually within four months. It tends to be aggressive, widely disseminated at diagnosis, and rapidly fatal.

What the hell can you do with information like that? I resort to magical thinking. *It won't happen to Ana. It won't.* And a grasp at logic: it's been three months already; is some of the danger past? Wouldn't there have been symptoms already? She has no lumps, no night sweats or weight loss. *It won't happen. It won't.*

But that night at our counseling session I'm more teary than usual. I realize why I've been focusing so much energy on Ana, on *us*; as she feels better, I want our relationship back, not just sex but romance. It hurts me that she seems so distant—not cold but distracted—much of the time. "You want a honeymoon," Betsy surmises, and it's true. But Ana is on her own journey, her focus more inward.

I think I shouldn't, but I do it anyway, I let it slip. "I read something at work today," I confess. And Betsy makes the link: the more frightened I am for Ana's health, the greater my sense of urgency that we connect. "It makes sense," she muses, "where you both are. Because let's say Ana *didn't* have a lot of time left. We don't know that to be true, but let's say it were true. Your task," she addresses me, "would be to let go of Ana. And your task," she turns to Ana, "would be to let go of the world."

Now Ana is starting on a new immunosuppressant drug, Cellsept; the doctors are signing her up as part of a research study. The informed consent form she brings home begins, "I understand that I have had a rejection episode which has not fully resolved, despite the use of standard medications. Therefore, I . . ."

"Is *that* what they think is going on? You're still in rejection?" I'm startled, disturbed. Ever since the OKT3 treatment Ana's creatinine has hovered in the mid-2s, a full point above normal. But the doctors kept saying not to worry, that as long as the count stayed stable, everything was fine; some people's counts never went all the way down: it might be because my kidney was small for her body, or the kidney might have been damaged just a little by the rejection episode. This happens, they told us over and over; nothing to be alarmed about. And for weeks I worried anyway, but then I began to get used to the numbers, to accept the doctors' explanations. And now, out of nowhere: *rejection not fully resolved.* Were they lying to us before? Have they changed their minds? "Your numbers are pretty good," Ana says the doctor told her, "but I think we can get them even better."

So she goes from the little figure eight–shaped yellow Imuran tablets to the shiny turquoise Cellsept capsules, and the next week her creatinine is 1.9. A few weeks after that it's 1.7, then 1.6, where it stays.

We're driving home from seeing *Jeffrey*, a bittersweet gay movie: boy meets boy, boy loses boy, boy gets boy again, but with a twist—it's the age of AIDS; boy #2 is HIV-positive, and boy #1 has to learn to deal with it. And finally he does. And the movie ends there, at the beginning—we assume—of their love. "Promise me you won't get sick. Promise me you won't die," says boy #1. "Done," says boy #2. "Liar," says boy #1, and they kiss. It's a happy ending, mostly, yet it leaves me sad—for what gay men have lost, for what Ana and I have lost.

It's near midnight, our car whistles along the empty highway with the lopsided moon—full just a few days ago—shining its high beam through the windshield, and somehow all this makes possible a different kind of conversation. "It's so wonderful," I say to Ana, "everything we can do now. The way we can park around the block from the movie theater and it's no big deal any more; you can walk. The little things."

"It's better than if I had HIV," says Ana. "At least I had this chance to get so much better. I have a different life now, but it's a good life."

"Yes." I squeeze her hand in the dark. There are tears on my cheeks. "Sometimes," I say, "sometimes I think maybe it's denial, because I know we went through a lot of hard stuff, but sometimes now I look back on it all and think, well, if that's as hard as it's going to get for a while, it wasn't *that* bad, you know? I mean, I could do it again, if I had to."

Ana groans. "Please, not me. You do it again, not me."

I'm crying through my laughter. "I told you, maybe it's denial, but denial is a useful thing sometimes too, you know? It's amazing," I say, "Everything that's happened. Do you remember when you told me you had diabetes? We were sitting there on the couch in my old house, and you were scared to tell me."

Ana nods.

"Imagine if you could have known then that within a few years you were going to need a kidney transplant, and I was going to give you a kidney." I don't know what I'm getting at, but it's got something to do with choices; four years ago, if I could have seen this future spooled out before me, I wouldn't have chosen it—as Dorey said, *I would not have chosen willingly to walk into the situation I'm now in.* And yet having arrived at this moment, I know there is no place else I would rather be.

⟳

Four months. How far we've come.

Ana is so much better, so much better, so much better. This is our refrain. And it is, undeniably, true. The foot ulcer is completely healed; she walks everywhere now, in her new five-hundred-dollar orthopedic shoes. She has more energy than I've seen her have in years—how many years? Two? Three? Her face is still Prednisone-plump; from that drug or one of the others her skin darkens quickly when exposed to sun. She's been wearing sunscreen, long sleeves, hats—all this because we know her risk of skin cancer is now dramatically increased—yet still she's summer-ruddy, and no matter what we know, she looks like the picture of health with this tan, everyone says so.

But I've been waiting for her to become again the person that she was. For us to take up, separately and together, where we left off. And some-times it seems we are doing that; we go through days, weeks now in an easy, unconscious summer pleasure. Each Saturday we shop at the Berke-ley farmer's market, a gentle hippie-run affair, for the freshest, ripest organic produce; we wheel our little red cart back to the car laden with fruit-sweet golden cherry tomatoes, raspberries, peaches, fragrant peppers and cilantro and basil; back at home I make vegetable and fruit salads, gua-camole and pesto, and we sit out on the deck in the sunshine savoring it all. We trim the dead blooms off our stolen roses, which are flourishing, and they bloom again. We plant new flowers in the front yard, refinish the floor of the deck, lie naked on the bed together under the spinning blades of the ceiling fan, bathed in a healthy, tired sweat—all this as if our lives were simple again.

It's the small things that remind us that Ana is different now. She's plucked the hairs that grew between her eyebrows, the ones she said made her look like Frida Kahlo, but there's still the hair fuzzing her arms, the sides of her face, the persistent mustache on her upper lip. And her body thermostat has changed; she used to get cold more easily than I did, and to tolerate heat much better—the logical result of growing up in Puerto Rico, we'd thought. Now we see how characteristics like these—these small, pre-dictable things one knows about oneself after a lifetime in the same body—are, after all, chemically based, subject to change. She's hardly ever cold now, but she can no longer bear the heat; some nights I lie under all the cov-ers while she lies on top of them, sweating, the fan on high.

And her bowels still aren't working right, despite all our efforts and the occasional temporary reprieve. She does everything the doctors say, and sometimes her stool is hard and sometimes it's soft, but either way it usu-ally doesn't come out on its own, so she carries the latex gloves and lubri-cant everywhere she goes.

And sexually, as far as I can tell, she's still not there. My attempts at seduction don't work; she laughs gently at me, brushes away my desire. When I try the blunt approach Betsy suggested, telling Ana directly that I'd like to make love, sometimes that gets through to her, and we do; but the love we make then is careful, deliberate, a wistful nod to the passion we once shared. She *tells* me she desires me, yet I feel no desire from her, only the plodding effort of her will. And I don't ever doubt that she loves me; but love and lust are not the same thing, and I want both from her.

Like her sensitivity to heat and cold, Ana's lust was a part of her I'd thought would never change. In the old days we'd made love not only when everything was right, but also when things were wrong—when we were rushed, or stressed, or in an inconvenient place. Once, when we had to get up very early to take Ana's sick brother to the airport—he was flying back to Puerto Rico for a last visit—we woke up even before the alarm went off. Five A.M. and our bodies were coming together in the dark, seeking what they could from each other; our sex then was brief and sad and perfect, silent and fierce. I'd thought after that that we shared a certain alchemy, an ability to transmute almost any feeling—fear or grief or despair, as well as longing—into the language of our bodies. I'd thought of that morning as proof that it would always be that way.

Now our planned, cautious comings-together depress me. They're so pallid compared to what was once possible between us, so different from what I miss and crave, that they seem almost worse than nothing at all. I argue with myself about this: *Just be grateful you have her here at all, alive and warm in your arms!* I try to be patient, to reign in my frustration. I remind myself of my certainty during the worst weeks: that even if this were to be all there was, even if our relationship could never again be sexual, my love was strong enough to survive. And I still feel that, although I also, when I think that this *is* all there is, all there will be, feel other things: self-pity, grief.

And so self-pity and grief are what I'm feeling the night before we leave for a four-day weekend trip, our first vacation—not counting Reno—since the surgery, a "last hurrah" before Ana goes back to work next week. It's been a full week since we've been sexual at all; I hate this shrewish counting of days. Yet all week I've been rubbing myself against Ana like a cat, putting her hands on my body, my hands on hers, and getting no response. I feel very, very sad.

But in the morning Ana has decided she wants to make love, to "start our trip off right," and I can't pull myself back from my sadness to her caresses. I lie there stiffly until she stops touching me. So now I'm angry at myself for missing this chance, angry at her for not giving it to me sooner, angry at our loss and how hard this has become—this once-simple dance.

"You used to . . . " I start, and of course it's the wrong thing to say.

"I hate it when you talk about the past!" Ana explodes. "It's like a parent who's always comparing one kid to their older sister or brother. 'Joe or Mary did this, Joe or Mary did that.' Well I'm *not* Joe or Mary; I'm me, and this is now!"

"But I'm *not* comparing you to someone else, I'm comparing you to *you*, I'm missing *you*," I wail. And then, shocked by the implications of what she's said: "Do you really feel so different from the person you used to be, that talking about the past feels like talking about someone else?"

"I don't know my own body any more," Ana says. "I used to know how I'd respond. What would turn me on. That's gone now."

And then she says, "I don't want you to think I'm not grateful. I'm very thankful, to you, to the doctors, to be living in a time when this was even possible. But you have to understand, I'm living with an organ now that's not *mine*, that I wasn't born with."

"And how does that make you feel?" Trying to get her to keep talking. "Is it a sense of—loss?" I venture, maybe because loss is what *I* feel so much of the time.

"No," Ana says with disgust, "It's a feeling of being invaded."

"It's like this," she adds after a minute. "It's like I'm buying a new car, making payments—that big pillbox over there, that's my payment—but I don't own the car, the bank does, and they could take it back from me at any time. Any time! Even though I'm making payments, it makes no difference. I could get cancer; my body could reject the kidney. Any time."

And later she says softly, "When you met me, I didn't have to take all these pills, check my sugar, watch what I ate and drank, worry about whether I would be able to shit. Sex used to be one of the most important things to me. It was a way to forget—no matter how bad I felt, I could have sex and I'd feel good. Now, with everything I'm dealing with, how can sex even matter to me? It's like a little, tiny corner of my life. Every once in a while I remember it: 'Oh, yes, my body can give me pleasure.' But I have to make an *effort* to remember."

"Sex doesn't work as a way for you to escape, now?" I ask, remembering how it used to seem to me that desire lived on the very surface of Ana's skin, so that she got aroused—we both did—at the barest touch.

"No," she says sadly. "It doesn't."

And, later, "I'll give you another example, a simple little example. I used to be able to walk on the beach barefoot, feel the sand between my toes. Now I can't do that—one, I can't feel the sand, because I have no sensation in my feet, and two, because it would be too risky: I could cut myself."

And I think, it doesn't really matter that the loss of sensation in her feet comes from the diabetes, not the transplant; what she's talking about is loss—loss after loss after loss—the cumulative sum of all of it together greater than each of the parts.

And in the bathroom, brushing my teeth and crying, grieving for Ana now as much as for myself, I think for the first time: *I want out. This is too big, too sad for me. I want out.*

It's a fleeting feeling, perfectly "normal," I know, and no real reflection of anything at all; but it's something I haven't ever said to myself before, even fleetingly. *I want out.*

⬥

Now I know what the phrase "the middle of nowhere" means. We're there.

Our cabin is an hour away from the nearest "city" (population 10,000), and 2½ miles down a steep, narrow dirt road from the nearest town (population 120). We're in a valley on the grounds of an abandoned gold mine; there are no other guests, just the proprietor—in the lodge down the hill— and us. There's a front and back porch, a nest of baby sparrows just above the front door, a squat black old-fashioned woodstove in the living room. There's a gurgling creek, its water heart-stoppingly cold. No TV, no telephone.

And here, so far removed from the reminders of Ana's illness, here on vacation like "normal" people once again, the traumas of the past six months seem even more unbelievable to us. And so, sprawled on the couch in the first evening's fading light, we play the Remembering Game.

"Remember the day you had the Thallium scan?" I ask. It was during the pre-transplant assessment of Ana's heart. She hadn't started dialysis yet; we were still hoping to avoid it entirely. She was too weak to go on the treadmill; I wheeled her through the hospital, pasty and dull-eyed, to the room where they would give her a radioactive contrast drug, then left her with her friend Mari, who'd shown up for moral support. I'd missed too much work already—that was my excuse; the truth was I couldn't bear any more, not that day, not that week. I drove off to work reassuring myself that anyway the procedure would be simple, non-invasive, painless.

In fact, Ana told me later, the doctors injected her with the contrast drug, as planned—but then, while they waited for it to be absorbed, they had her sit still, arm raised, while they snapped film from angle after angle. Ana's gout or pseudo-gout, whatever it was that caused her such devastating body aches before the transplant, made the process an agony for her. She did what the doctors told her to do, crying the whole time. And Mari talked and begged and coaxed her through it, teasing and joking and distracting in her rapid-fire English and Spanish—*loca* Mari the free spirit, the clown, who proved her friendship that day as never before. When I heard from Ana later what the day had been like I felt both guilty and terribly relieved not to have been there.

"Remember everything that went wrong?" I ask. "When my blood came back ambiguous for hepatitis B, and they ordered a retest, and the administrative assistant ordered the wrong test so we waited ten days for nothing? And then they had to send it to a lab out of state, so we waited another two weeks. Then we did the 24-hour urine collection, and I brought it to the hospital, and they spilled it, so we had to do it again."

Ana laughs. "And Helena, the transplant coordinator. She really bugged you."

"Of course she bugged me! I was so frantic, trying to get everything done as fast as possible, trying to keep you off dialysis, and every time I talked to her she'd say in that patronizing way of hers, 'A kidney transplant is *not* an emergency procedure.' Well, to us it *was* an emergency!"

But we're far enough past that now that I can laugh too, even as I kiss Ana's tear in its silent path down her cheek. "Of course, I bugged her too. I memorized the phone number she gave me once, which she usually didn't give out; I called her practically every day. No one else called her at that number, so she always knew it was me when she picked up the phone."

"Remember when they thought you had cancer?" Ana says.

"They thought there was a 'remote possibility' I had cancer," I correct her. My kidney x-ray had picked up a tiny spot in my right kidney, a spot the radioactive dye had for some reason not filled, and the doctors weren't sure why. They repeated the test, got the same result. The next step would be a more invasive test—they'd have to give me general anesthesia, poke a scope through my urethra and bladder all the way into the kidney, so they could look around. They didn't want to do that until they knew for sure Ana was a candidate for transplant, which meant she had to have a coronary angiogram first, to further explore the heart abnormalities they'd found on her thallium scan. But they couldn't do the angiogram until after Ana had started dialysis; her kidney function was poor enough by that time that it would just be too risky otherwise, they said. So we were stuck: no angiogram, no transplant. No dialysis, no angiogram. Ana had to do what she'd sworn she'd never do.

Ana muses, "Remember the night I started dialysis? That was the worst night of my life."

She'd decided she wanted to do peritoneal dialysis; it seemed the lesser evil, because at least she could do it at home. But she was too weak and sick for them to be able to implant the necessary tube into her peritoneum safely; they decided they'd have to dialyze her another way for a few weeks first. So, in what we were assured would be a "quick, painless outpatient procedure," Ana would have two plastic IV hookups inserted into the large clavial vein in her neck. "Can I stay in the room with her while they do it?" I'd asked worriedly, and the nurse had soothed me, "Sure, sure you can."

But when the doctor came in he asked me to leave; it made him nervous to have someone watching, he said. I waited and waited in the small, cell-like waiting room across the hall; finally, after forty-five minutes I snuck back to the windowed corridor outside the room where Ana lay, and stood there and eavesdropped. It seemed the procedure had been harder than the doctor expected; I heard him telling the nurse that the skin on Ana's neck was tough. I saw Ana lying still on the table, her face and hair covered by surgical caps to protect her from the blood that could splash up as they entered the large vein; then the doctor turned around and, afraid of being seen, I slunk back into the waiting room, angry with myself for doing so.

A few minutes later it was over. They wheeled Ana out on a gurney; she looked dazed, the two big tube portals protruding from her neck like a turkey's wattles. When I asked if it had hurt, she just looked at me—numb or furious, I wasn't sure which.

"A lot?" I asked.

"Yes."

Slowly, gingerly, we transferred her from the gurney into her wheelchair, and I wheeled her through the halls to the hemodialysis unit.

The first thing that struck both of us there was the sickly-sweet chemical smell. Patients lay still on reclining chairs draped with white sheets, blood flowing from their veins into a set of long, thin loops of tube. Filled with deep red fluid, the tubes looked like crazy straws, I thought wildly. I watched as a nurse hooked Ana up to one of the machines, the "kidney," as the other patients called it, watched as the straws filled up with her blood, carried it to the machine, then back into her veins, and I thought, *I hope I will never, ever get used to this.*

"That was the night the guy was dying in there," Ana says.

"No, it wasn't that night, it was a few days later. When we went back on Saturday. Remember? Because that day they put you on the other side of the room, near his corner," I insist.

The man had been lying on a gurney, covered with a sheet, and his voice was so high and thin that at first we weren't sure of his sex. "Oh God," he moaned over and over. "Oh, God. Oh, God. Ohhhhhhhhhhhhhhhh, Godddddd."

"He has AIDS," a nurse told us, brisk and apologetic at once. "He's dying."

"Then why—?"

"His wife won't let us take him off dialysis. She wants to keep him alive." She turned to go. "Actually," she added, not looking at us, "I think she wants him to suffer."

He sounded like he was suffering, all right. Ana turned on the little TV set near her, trying to tune out. I sat cross-legged on the floor beside her chair, trying to concentrate on the previous week's Sunday paper.

"You're right," says Ana now. "The dying man was on Saturday. Remember when I started on peritoneal dialysis?"

One week after Ana began hemodialysis the doctors agreed to implant the tube in her peritoneum, though she wouldn't be able to use it for two weeks more. The surgery was scheduled for 7:00 A.M., and they instructed us to be at the hospital at 6:00. Always a night person, one who reads, prowls, cleans, writes till early morning for my own sanity, I'd barely slept. I stayed with Ana in the same-day surgery area while she was prepped, but just before 7:00, when they wheeled her away, I was cut loose; I'd meant to spend the next few hours concentrating on her well-being, sending her telepathic messages of strength and hope and love, but I was just too tired, too scared and sad. I wandered down into the hospital lobby, but I felt trapped there, confined, so I walked on out into the gray morning, thick with San Francisco spring fog. A few blocks from the hospital I found a hilly park, a bench; I stretched out there and napped, using my handbag as a pillow, until the fog burned off and the rising sun shone straight on my face. It was 9:00; the hospital had said Ana wouldn't be in her room until at least 11:00. I got up, walked aimlessly up and down the street, looking in the windows of the trendy stores; the lives they represented, catered to, with their expensive antiques and gourmet foods and fine jewelry, seemed a million miles from my own. Finally I sat down on a sunny patch of sidewalk near the hospital, made myself comfortable with my water bottle and a notebook, and tried to write. Passersby looked at me curiously, trying to size me up.

I wrote,

For what do we pour out so much love?
Is the universe a cup,
that it can catch and hold it and make use of it,
as it flows by the lips of those
it cannot save, flows over . . . ?

At 11:00 I went back inside to check at the hospital volunteers' desk; no, no word yet about Ana. At 11:30 I went back again; still no word. I began to get anxious. I imagined Ana dead, tried to envision grieving, then re-creating my life without her. At noon I returned to the desk. "They often start the surgeries behind schedule," the elderly volunteer explained to me, kindly. "This delay doesn't mean that anything is wrong."

At 12:30, finally, I heard that Ana was being moved up to a room. I rushed up to the ward; she hadn't arrived yet, but they were expecting her. At last an orderly wheeled her down the hall, and I ran to her, kissed her forehead and cheeks and neck as she rode. She was sleepy and weak, but hungry, so I fed her some clear broth. Then I stayed with her a few hours more, then headed home for a few hours to feed the animals, shower, nap, try to remember who I was—before driving back to the hospital again to bring her home.

"Do you still think it was worth it, going on peritoneal dialysis?" I ask Ana now. As it turned out, the transplant was done only six weeks later.

"Definitely," Ana nods. "Hemodialysis was so depressing, all those people lying around like they were dead! It was so *passive*. At least with peritoneal dialysis I had some control."

But I remember it differently. Before we could get the dialysis machine in our house Ana had had to go through two weeks of one-on-one training with a nurse, learning more than she'd ever wanted to know about the anatomy of the peritoneum, the importance of sterile technique, the vagaries of the equipment. During the weeks when Ana walked around miserable from the hemodialysis tubes in her neck we'd thought it would be better to have her dialyze at home, at night—"more convenient, more comfortable, more empowering," as the literature said. But the sickly-sweet smell of the dialysis unit followed us home in the bags of fluid she emptied into the toilet every morning, and the process made her feel isolated, alien; in the hemodialysis unit I'd been her lover, her ally, but now I was simply the unfathomably healthy person on the other side of the chasm that had opened up in our bed. Even on the nights when the machine's alarm didn't get tripped, Ana lay awake for hours, her body aching and tense, and watched me and the cats and dogs as we all slept—and in the worst of those moments she hated us for it.

"For me the ureteroscopy was the worst. Worse than the transplant surgery itself," I say. The scope didn't reveal anything new. The doctors never did figure out what had caused the "filling defect" on my kidney x-ray; when they peered around inside my kidney, everything looked fine. But the scope itself irritated the kidney so much that the doctor put in a stent after he was done, a little metal tube to hold open the passageway between the kidney and the ureter, and he left me catheterized for the weekend, "just to avoid any problems." All weekend I limped awkwardly around, sore from both the procedure and the catheter.

On Monday morning the doctor removed the stent, then deflated the little balloon that had held the catheter inside me, and Ana and I took off down the street to get a Mother's Day present for my mom. But within half an hour I knew that something was very wrong. There was a throbbing, pulsing, cramping pain on my right side, just below my kidney, a pain so severe I finally lay down on the store's carpeted floor, trying to hold still, willing it to pass. It didn't; it got worse, far worse than any pain I'd ever felt. Walking was better than sitting or lying, I discovered. I stumbled back up the street to the hospital, paced back and forth in the doctor's office, in his examining room.

"The ureter's cramping, that's all," he told me, shaking his head. "Happens sometimes. It's the kind of pain where you can't sit still, right?"

Writhing on the floor by that time, I nodded up at him. His face was kind, concerned, helpless.

"At the E.R. they can give you some Demerol," he offered finally.

The Demerol didn't help. The nurse asked me to rate my pain on a scale of 1 to 10, with 10 being the worst pain I could imagine; I gave it a 9 when I walked in the door, and a half-hour after my Demerol shot it was still a 7 or 8. I squirmed uncontrollably in my hospital bed, sitting up, lying down, getting up to pace some more.

"The doctor said we can give you some morphine, too," the nurse finally reported back. Obediently I lowered my pants for the shot. Slowly, slowly, as the opiate took effect, the pain began to diminish. When I finally floated out of the E.R. I rated it a 3 or so, and I felt so high and strange it hardly seemed to matter.

That afternoon I sat out in the backyard, talking on the phone to Helena, the transplant coordinator. As always, there was another detail to be worked out. Suddenly I told her I had to go. A minute later I vomited all over the deck.

Later that night, lying in bed, I began to shake. Ana piled blankets on top of me, but nothing helped; teeth chattering, I quivered under their weight. "Must be an infection," the doctor said when we reached him. "Happens sometimes." I took some antibiotics we had in the house, and he ordered more for me. By morning the shaking had stopped, but the cramping pain continued, on and off, for the rest of the week, never again as intense as it had been the first time, but still bad. When it came I propped myself up with hot water bottles, front and back; one night at midnight, desperate, I went out to the hot tub, kicking underwater until the spasms lessened.

At the end of that week our transplant surgery was performed.

"It's been a hell of a six months," I say now. The creek runs steadily below our window.

"*Pero ya estamos aquí,*" says Ana. *We're here now.*

The next morning when we wake up, the cabin is freezing; here at 3,500 feet the temperature drops dramatically at night, even in August. I pull on a turtleneck and sweatpants, let the dogs out, and build a fire; then we huddle around the flames, wishing we'd brought oatmeal for breakfast instead of cold cereal and fruit. But then within a few hours it's warm—too warm; the woodstove is still steaming away, so we open all the cabin's windows. Baby birds are chirping just outside the door. We dive back into bed naked, wriggling against the deliciously cool sheets, against each others' bodies.

Just as if none of it had ever happened.

Because it has all happened, *y ya estamos aquí.*

We make love, and it's almost, though not quite, like old times.

There are butterflies everywhere here, huge lacy white ones with green markings, pausing to sun themselves on rocks or balancing, light on light, on the tiny wildflowers. The dogs dash ahead of us on the little dirt road, wildly exuberant, wiping out any chance we might have had to see other wildlife; but the butterflies are unfazed.

We've been hoping lately that Ana's constipation may be getting better. She did go, finally, to see a G.I. specialist, who recommended only that she eat a high-fiber cereal every day. The cereal makes her stool bulkier, but it doesn't do much to help it leave her body. "So much for high-tech medicine," I comment wryly. If doctors' advice was all we had available, we'd be up a creek; their help couldn't heal the hole on Ana's foot, nor, it seems, can they get her shit to come out on its own. But fortunately we're exploring other avenues as well. My cousin recommended high-dose magnesium, which she takes nightly and swears by, so Ana has used that for the past couple of weeks. And so far the combination, the three daily stool softeners *plus* the cereal *plus* the magnesium, seems to have made a difference; she's going to the bathroom normally about half the time now, and the rest of the time she gives herself just a little help with the glove. It's an improvement.

At dinnertime we walk down the dusty road to the lodge, where the proprietor cooks for us. Our cabin has a kitchen, so we prepare our own breakfasts and lunches, but having dinner at the lodge saves us some work and lends a structure to the day. At 7:00 P.M. sharp he rings the dinner bell—"It's a custom," he explains, grinning, when I point out that it's hardly necessary; we're the only guests here right now, and we're already in the lodge. He's a strange guy, a bit wild-eyed, but soft-spoken and courteous; he lives all alone up here, with no regular company but his dogs, and serves as handyman, cook, chambermaid, and gardener all at once. He tells us about his plans to rebuild the deck; meanwhile he's fixing up the cabins, one by one.

"Is this your place?" I ask him, trying to understand what would motivate a man to live so completely alone.

"You mean, am I the owner? Nah, just the caretaker." He sees my curiosity. "I used to come up here back in the seventies, when I was still drinking, needed to chill out a little. Then when I got sober I figured this would be a good place to land."

He's a decent cook; he's made us some kind of broiled fish, plus salad, rolls, boiled new potatoes, and sautéed zucchini, plus cherry pie for dessert. It's a feast just for the two of us, since he serves us and then retreats to the kitchen. It's a strange feeling, this kind of luxury here in the midst of such rough land, but we try to make the most of it.

"*Brindemos*," I say to Ana. *Let's toast.*

"*Brindemos, pues. A nuestro amor.*" *To our love.*

"And to your health," I add, clinking my water glass against hers.

"And yours." We clink.

"To sex and passion, *que tengamos mucho, para siempre.*" *May we have a lot of it, always.*

"*A nuestros futuros, que sean llenos de luz,*" says Ana. *May our futures be filled with light.*

On our way back up the road at twilight, the dogs careening eagerly behind us, a butterfly hovers close. We've seen them nearby before, but this one flutters around and around us, doing figure eights, first around Ana, then around me.

"She's trying to tell us something," I say, only half joking.

Ana stops to catch her breath on the incline, turns around to face the way we've come. The butterfly lands on her abdomen and stays there, breathing, flexing its pale wings.

"She's telling me that my intestinal system is going to work better now," Ana says matter-of-factly. "That I won't be battling with the constipation much longer."

Still the butterfly remains on Ana's stomach, light as a blessing.

"*Gracias, mariposita*," Ana thanks it, and it flies off then, though it remains close to us the rest of the way to our cabin.

⬥

"Do you realize you haven't gotten a single mosquito bite?" I ask Ana later, scratching at mine. The bugs here are ferocious, mosquitoes and flies and tiny gnats that aim straight for our eyes.

"That's true," Ana says wonderingly. We've been using insect repellent, but still it's striking that she hasn't been bitten once. Eight months ago, on our last trip to Puerto Rico before the transplant, Ana had suffered terribly from her mosquito bites. While they were an annoyance to me, they were an absolute torture for her; she scratched herself until there were bleeding sores all over her body, until we sought out a doctor who gave her a cortisone shot. She'd never been that badly affected by mosquitoes before; we figured it must have had something to do with her kidney failure, the toxins in her blood. We were so close then to the end.

"Now the mosquitoes don't like me," Ana muses. "Maybe it's the medications."

"We've just discovered the one and only *positive* side effect," I laugh. "But is it that you don't *taste* good any longer, or that your immune system doesn't respond to the bites?"

Ana shrugs. "Either way, I'm not complaining."

I keep scratching.

Later, in our next support group meeting, we'll hear this confirmed. No one post-transplant gets mosquito bites any more.

"You know that old expression," someone starts. "Every cloud . . ."

"Has a silver lining!" the rest of us chant in unison.

⬥

At work, when the latest medical journals hit my In Box, I read about a man who had four episodes of acute rejection in the first seven weeks following his kidney transplant.

Wow, I think, *we're lucky.*

I read about a woman who had one rejection episode, and got over it; after that, her kidney functioned fine for three months. Then she went into rejection again; this time it didn't respond to the medications, and the kidney had to be removed.

I wonder, *Is it too soon to know how lucky we are?*

Then I read about a current medical controversy: new evidence has indicated that calcium channel blockers, a class of blood pressure medications, may actually *increase* the risk of heart attack. Doctors use medication to lower people's blood pressure because studies have shown that people with high blood pressure are more prone to heart attacks; but blood pressure is what they call a "surrogate marker," I understand now, not necessarily significant in itself, and they're finding that these things don't work as neatly as they once imagined. Some drugs may lower blood pressure yet have no impact at all on cardiac mortality; some, it seems now, may even increase mortality.

I read more closely. The culprit drug is called Nifedipine. For some reason that name rings a bell, so I look it up in the PDR, and there it is: *marketed under the name Procardia*. In the highest dose studied, 80 mg. per day, patients had three times more heart attacks than people on other blood pressure medications; Ana, on four pills a day, had been taking 120 mg.

How long have they known about this? Furiously, I search through all the medical journals in the office. "Too soon to draw conclusions," one editorial pontificates. "National Institutes of Health issues warning," informs another. "Doctors advised to use alternative antihypertensives." Finally I find what I'm looking for, what I suspected: the results of this study were first made public in March, two months before Ana's transplant.

Why? Why did her doctors prescribe the Procardia at all? Why did they quadruple her dose? Why didn't I think to look up the medication then? Why didn't I know everything? Why didn't the doctors? *Shouldn't* they know everything? Shouldn't they at least have known about *this?*

I'm chilled by my own questions, by this reminder of our vulnerability. I don't believe the doctors are malicious; I can't afford to believe that. But Ana is my lover, not theirs. No one will ever be as concerned for her as I am. When the doctors first gave Ana the Procardia, she'd just gone through her rejection episode; we were so terrified and grateful, and I'd already asked so many questions, the last thing I would have thought to question was the blood pressure medication. Yet now it seems that that's exactly what I should have questioned. That I should, must, question everything.

FIVE

The hotline is exactly twenty minutes from my house on days when there's no traffic anywhere along the route. My co-workers carpool, but none of them live near me, and I'm secretly glad: driving alone means I can time the trip as tight as I want to, almost inevitably arriving just a few minutes late; besides, I enjoy the time alone in the car. I listen to Spanish radio, singing along with the passionate *baladas*, the lusty torch songs, the country western–style predictability of the lyrics.

> *No necesariamente, tiene que ser legítimo,*
> *pero quiero que tú me ames, y que sea recíprico . . .*
> *Quiero que me hagas el amor—*

> *It doesn't necessarily have to be legitimate,*
> *but I want you to love me, and for it to be reciprocal . . .*
> *I want you to make love to me—*

One afternoon I hear the song I always think of as Ana's and my song, a hit from a few years back. It was playing on the radio in the appliance store the day we went to pick out a washer and dryer for our new house.

> *Me estoy enamorando hoy de ti, pero perdidamente;*
> *Yo que tanto decía que jamás me volvería a pasar.*
> *Me estoy enamorando hoy de ti, pero desesperadamente;*
> *Yo no lo esperaba, pero te amo cada día más.*

I'm falling in love with you today, completely,
I who had so often said this would never happen to me again.
I'm falling in love with you today, desperately,
I didn't expect this, but I love you more each day.

With the song's sweetly romantic lyrics, with the mundane, domestic, symbolic purchase that reflected the joining of our lives in a way Ana and I had never expected to join them, both Ana's and my eyes had filled with tears. We sniffled as we signed the papers for the delivery. "Romantic fools," Ana muttered as we left the store, and we both laughed.

How fragile that time seems to me now, how innocent, and how inexorably doomed. We moved into the house in May, and that August, when Ana was hospitalized for a foot ulcer, her doctor called in a nephrologist. That was when we learned that her kidneys were on their way out, that it wouldn't be long—though the doctor guessed two or three years, and in fact it was less than two.

It's on my drive home from work, watching the sky move through fog and sunset above me, that I remember I'm still the same person I've always been. I drove cross-country alone at age sixteen, balancing cups of truck-stop coffee and oatmeal cookies between the stick shift and the emergency brake of my vw bug, and I got hooked on the romance of the road then, the freedom of being alone in my car on the highway, any highway. I could go anywhere, I think. *I could be anyone.* For many years I'd nurtured an image of myself as rootless, a gypsy, as if I could start my life over again, any place, any time I chose.

I had never intended to commit myself to Ana. When we met I was one year out of a seven-year relationship; I meant to date, to explore, and I told her that from the beginning. I told her, too, that I would never fall in love with her; she was different than anyone else I'd been with, and her intensity both intrigued and frightened me.

After we had dated for a year, I left Ana and went to South America, on a trip I'd planned since long before I met her. I'd been working in aids education for six years then, and I thought I needed a change. I wanted to improve my Spanish, to live cheaply and write a great deal; I also wanted, as I wrote to a friend, to "throw all the pieces of my life into the air to see how and where they'll land." I intended to stay for at least six months, possibly a year or longer; I paid extra for an airline ticket with an open return date.

"So are we breaking up?" Ana asked insistently as I packed.

"No, I don't want to break up. But I don't want to make any promises either. I don't know how long I'm going to be in Ecuador. I may want to be with other people there."

"So we're breaking up, then." There were tears in her eyes, but her voice was resolute.

"No, I don't want to break up with you. I just don't want to make any promises."

Somehow Ana tolerated those painful months of mixed messages from me, my leave-taking, and then my absence. I don't believe I could have done the same in her place; hurt, anger, pride would have forced me to close her from my heart. And yet, hurt, angry, proud, Ana waited for me. At first, I saw this as a weakness in her. Now I have come to understand it differently, as an outpouring of faith.

And in Ecuador, thousands of miles away, I missed Ana desperately. I made friends and told them about her; I heard music in cafés, thought of Ana and cried. We talked often on the phone, hundreds of dollars' worth of conversations in which she urged me to stay, to explore, to do what I'd gone there to do—while I wept, longing to hold her, to feel her lips on my skin. I spent my thirtieth birthday walking alone through a park in downtown Quito, thinking of all the years I'd wanted to do this, how much I'd given up in order to do it—and wondering why.

And so, after three months away, I returned to San Francisco and to Ana.

My time away had not been easy for Ana. Her brother Adrian had died just a few months before I left. While I was gone she parted ways with someone who had been a close friend. And she was hospitalized twice, once for an infection, the second time for an allergic reaction to antibiotics. She had gained weight. Her angina had worsened, and it appeared that she might need heart surgery. I knew, finally, that I loved her. I also knew her future would be difficult.

Less than two months after my return I was offered a month-long consulting job in Africa, helping to establish an AIDS hotline in Swaziland. Next, I was invited to serve as a writer-in-residence at the University of Wisconsin for the coming academic year. It would mean a chance to write, to gain teaching experience, to be paid well for starting a new kind of life. And I knew that many people sustain long-distance relationships for months or even years. At first I planned to take the job and to return to San Francisco for monthly visits. "It's not that long a time," friends assured me. Yet I feared that Ana's health would worsen over that period of time, and I didn't want to be thousands of miles away if it did.

I went to Africa, worked and wrote and missed Ana. And on the twenty-six-hour plane ride home I realized my decision was already made. I would not go to Wisconsin. I would stay in the Bay Area and build a life with Ana instead.

Sometimes on the highway now, when I turn the radio up loud and the sky stretches wide before me, I think about the year I didn't spend in Wisconsin. I picture the apartment I might have rented, just a block or two from the lake; I would have skated or skied on that lake, would have invited my students home for potlucks. I imagine seeing myself through their eyes as a Writer, capital W. That year, and whatever direction my life might have taken after that, floats beneath my life still as a kind of shadow-life, the one I turned away from; I miss it sometimes, wistfully, though I have never regretted the choice I made.

These days when people ask me how I am, I answer automatically again. I'm fine. After all, the crisis has passed. Yet when someone pauses, leaving open that space that implies that they want to know how I *really* am, I don't know what to do. "Fine," I repeat. "I'm fine." Sometimes I add that Ana is doing well, that she's back at work, not even using the wheelchair any more. It's so much easier to talk about Ana than about myself.

Occasionally, if someone catches me in a more pensive mood, I might say, "It's like waking up from a long, confusing, disturbing dream—you know, that feeling of disorientation? I'm trying to remember who I am, where I left my life, so I can go back and pick up where I left off. Wondering if I *want* to go back and pick up where I left off, or if I'm someone different now, if I want a different life."

On the outside, I still look solid; my co-workers have complimented me on how well I continued to function, even through the worst months of the crisis. That's what I like about this job: all I have to do is bring my body here in the morning, and the work takes over from there. I have a highly efficient autopilot setting.

But I don't really *want* to be on autopilot any more. I want to remember how to get back to the control panel—I think.

Ana is a dynamo these days. Now that the foot ulcer has finally healed, she's been cooking more, doing most of the dishes too; when I protest, she reminds me how long I did everything. She's taken charge of the garden, waters it faithfully every afternoon. She hardly watches TV any more, doesn't read the paper; I haven't heard a word about her stamp collection in weeks. She cleared off six months' worth of paperwork at her job in her first week back. She's bustling, active, efficient, cheerful; this is how she gets *her* life back, from the outside in, while I seem to work the other way around. "I feel useful again," she says.

At the same time, she's become a crusader. She's constantly exhorting her diabetic sister to control her infections, monitor her blood sugar, take insulin if necessary. "See a second doctor," she tells her. "See a third, a fourth." *Otherwise you'll end up like me*, the subtext goes. "Take vitamin E. Take fish oil."

An old friend of Ana's, also diabetic, calls from another state. No, she doesn't test her sugar, she tells Ana; it's too hard, she's got too much else on her mind. "Anyway," the friend adds glibly, "they can always give me a kidney transplant, just like they did for you. Maybe they'll give me a new pancreas too, so I won't be diabetic any more."

"*Pendeja!* As if it were that simple," Ana rages when she gets off the phone.

"Do you think there's anything anyone could have said to you that would have made a difference all those years ago?" I ask. "Anything that would've made you change?"

Ana pauses in her tirade, considers my question. "No," she says finally.

⸙

I try to reach Julia again, leaving one, two, three messages. Finally there's a new message on her answering machine: it's Steve's voice now, back from the dead. When Julia calls me back she confirms he's almost back to normal. "It must've been meningitis, after all." Her new poems, when she sends them, are a litany of gratitude. *No lessons to learn*, she had said; but they say otherwise.

⸙

It's Saturday morning again, two weeks since we left the cabin. Since we've been back, sex has felt impossible again. Yet last night, at a birthday party for one of her friends, Ana was ribald; always rowdy and coarse in a Puerto Rican crowd, she was even more so this time, almost vulgar. As her friend opened her presents, Ana kept joking that there would be a vibrator in one of the boxes. She joked, too, about what the friend and her partner would do when all the guests had left. She called one of the other women there a nymphomaniac. Finally someone else, in the same joking tone, commented that maybe the people who talk most about sex are those who do it least. *Bingo*, I thought.

Ana tells me that she misses making love. But I'm tired of always being the one to try to initiate it, the perpetually disappointed, aggrieved one: I've decided to let her be the one who makes it happen.

When she tries, it's that just that: a trial, an effort. Her breasts are painful—from the Cellcept? or from these hormonal changes no one can explain? Her skin is very sensitive; I pinch her lightly, just a squeeze of a caress, and she says it hurts. She tells me how *not* to touch her, but not what still feels good; she lies motionless under my touch, willing herself to respond. Piña the calico cat comes between us then, purring and kneading the crumpled sheets, our bodies; we throw her off the bed and she jumps back up. The phone rings; we don't answer it, but the answering machine is turned up loud enough that we can hear the message being left. The tiny flicker of passion we were reaching for sputters, like a wet candle, and goes out.

"I wish I had my old sexuality back," Ana says, and there are tears on her cheeks.

Afterward we lie silent in defeat, our legs tangled together, Ana's big head heavy on my chest, and I think about her first nephrologist, Dr. Klinefeld. He was in his early sixties, silver-haired, prominent in the field; he traveled all over the world giving talks on dialysis; he spoke with a slow, drawn-out, affected gentility. And most of what he told us was untrue.

A few months after Ana began seeing him I had asked him about the low-protein diets I'd read about as a way to forestall kidney failure. "Oh, no, it's much too late for that," he responded; a low-protein diet at this point wouldn't help, might even hurt, he said.

Months later, once Ana was on dialysis, I finally went to the health library I'd been meaning to go to for so long. There I read about people who started on low-protein diets when their kidneys were far worse than Ana's had been when I brought up the question; I read how they'd staved off dialysis or transplantation for years, keeping their kidney function stable, even improving it a little. I read all this while Ana lay in her recliner in the big room with the sickly-sweet smell, her blood looped around her body in crazy straw tubes, and the dying man moaned in the corner.

Dr. Klinefeld also explained that Ana would be on dialysis for at least six months after her kidneys failed; there was no point in even thinking about potential kidney donors before that time, he said. I was the one who found out otherwise, who contacted the transplant center; if our timing had been luckier, perhaps if the doctor hadn't misled us so about how long Ana's kidneys would last—if he'd been honest, said "they *may* last another two to three years, or they may begin to fail at any time; put whatever arrangements you can in place, so you'll be prepared"—she could have avoided dialysis altogether.

Of course, I imagine that Dr. Klinefeld didn't mean to lie to us; he just didn't know what we needed to know, and didn't tell us so. "Oh yes, reduced libido is a symptom of failing kidneys," he acknowledged when I asked—what a huge relief it was then, hearing that. Then he added, practically winking at us, "The good news is, that will change after the transplant." Just that one phrase—what hope it kindled in me! Crazy though it seems now, I'd imagined Ana's desire returning full-force, and instantly. We'd heard inspiring stories, people just a day post-transplant who said they hadn't even remembered what it was like to feel so good; they weren't talking about sex, of course, but I'd extrapolated, joked about jumping on top of Ana right there in her hospital bed.

Now I look at Ana's body so gorgeous and fat and full, the woman I adore stretched naked before me—essentially untouchable, unreachable. Heavy with sadness, we go to the shower, and I watch as Ana soaps herself up, lathers her hair, scrubs and vigorously rinses; and I wonder again how I can ever comprehend what has been taken from us, what has been given back. I remember how a few months ago I had to wash her and dry her like a baby; she was too weak, in too much pain, to do these simple things. And I think of the woman I fell in love with four and a half years ago, the woman I gave my kidney to bring back—how she is both here and not-here now, only partly returned from the underworld.

❦

Still we go to the farmer's market every Saturday morning: a ritual of sunshine and health, a celebration of sweetness as summer draws to a close. The tables are piled high with squash and peppers and raspberries, the stuff of life itself, here for the taking, fresh and ripe. Street musicians play beside the stalls, their guitar cases open for coins; we pause between the peaches to listen, to bask a while in their blues.

One Saturday in August there's a Cajun festival at the market, and after we fill our little red cart with produce I urge Ana toward the crowd gathered around the stage, the people whirling and stomping, flushed with music. She resists. "We were going to weed the garden."

"We can do that later. Come on, I just want to hear the music for a little while."

She goes, but reluctantly. I perch on a low stone wall, dancing with the upper half of my body, hugging Ana between songs; and she stands there, stiff and unrelenting, until bit by bit the how-Berkeley-can-you-be crowd begins to win her over: the old man with the long white beard, dressed all in tie-dye, spinning by himself; the couple dancing with their poodle, handing the dog back and forth between docey-does; the children waving their arms above their heads like sunflowers, swaying in the center of the group. Onstage a man who has strapped a metal washboard to his chest runs a stick back and forth over its ridges, turning it into a southern version of the *guiro*, the ridged gourd played in Puerto Rico; a woman pumps away on a bright red accordion, and the guy playing percussion brings his hands down on his instruments with all the serious abandon of an orchestra conductor, dreamy and fierce.

I hop off the wall and begin to dance around Ana, moving my hands around her body, willing her to join in. Slowly, tentatively, she does. Then the music takes her and she lets it, she's dancing; just like before, she takes my shoulders and hips in her hands and leads my body, making it follow hers, an ecstatic fusion.

Later she admits, "I'd forgotten I could dance. I mean, I'd forgotten that I could actually do it and feel okay. That it doesn't tire me out the way it used to."

"Is that why you didn't want to go over there, at first?" At last I understand her reluctance, which I'd misread as stubbornness.

"Well, you know," she shrugs, "if all you can do is stand there, it's not much fun."

"But you can dance now," I remind her, hugging her. "*Mi bailadora.*"

Reclaiming, still reclaiming what was lost. So many losses we had never even acknowledged.

Another weekend we spend all day Saturday, after our farmer's market trip, rearranging our living room. We've lived in the house for two and a half years but barely use the room; there's just too much in it: a jumble of plants and knickknacks and posters and Ana's huge fish tank. Ana empties half the water out of the tank, but even so we can barely move it. She braces my feet with hers so I can push with my ass, and the whole thing slides a little; then we switch and she crouches low and pushes with her shoulder, like a goat. Slowly, together, we get it to the other side of the room. After that the tall stereo cabinet's a snap, practically feather-light. We take pictures off the wall, nail them back up in different places. We sweep the floor, fuss over the new arrangements, moving a plant an inch or two back and forth until it seems just perfect to us both. We're exhausted and stiff when we finish, but very pleased with ourselves.

Afterward, sitting in the hot tub, I name the feeling that has been growing in me for weeks now, even stronger since Ana returned to work: *I no longer know the direction our lives are moving in.* Which is a good thing, in a way, but also strange—like a big piece of open sky in front of me again. I see now that for years we've constructed our lives, consciously and unconsciously, around the knowledge that her health was going to get worse, that things were going to go in one direction only: downhill.

"Now I'm starting to think differently," I say. "Of course, we don't know for sure, but it's starting to feel like your health may stay the way it is now for a long time. It may even get better."

"I feel a sense of control again," she says. "In my work—having authority over people's lives. Not that I want to use it in a bad way; just the opposite. But it feels good to have that power again."

"It changes the way you think about yourself," I say, and she agrees.

"But what I'm talking about is the way we both think about our *lives*, the assumptions we don't even think about, yet base all our decisions on, like your not wanting to go hear the Cajun music, only on a larger scale."

She nods.

"When we were first together, you told me you didn't think you'd live to be forty," I say. She is forty-one now. "For a long time, I've believed that—believed that your time was very limited. I've thought about what I would do after you died. Now it's starting to occur to me that you really may *not* die any time soon. Your heart's not in the greatest shape, but it's not that bad. And we don't have any guarantees, but this kidney *may* last you a very long time. It's a different way to think about everything." I feel myself taking another slow, tentative step with each word I speak.

Ana has often talked about wanting to go back to school, to get a graduate degree and become a therapist. "You'd be so great at that," I tell her. "And there are so few therapists who are bilingual. And with all the experience you've had . . ."

But she's hesitant, not ready to attach herself to that dream yet. She wants a holding pattern now, wants to live a regular life for a while: to go to work every day, stop and do errands on the way home, take care of the house, the animals, the garden.

"I can take early retirement in nine years," she says.

"You could take a disability retirement any time. You know, even if you *weren't* really completely disabled, with your health history you could justify it."

She nods, considering. But she knows what she wants for right now, and big change isn't it. I'm the one always looking to expand, to shake things up, to build higher and higher onto my life until it threatens to topple over.

And what do *I* want now? "You know how it is," I joke with friends. "Now that Ana's health is better, I just have to go back to all the usual angst."

For a long time I'd wondered if perhaps, in a strange way, Ana's illness had made it easier for me to commit myself to her. I'd thought of myself as restless, a perpetual seeker; I'd always struggled with the idea of choosing just one lover, one house, one city, one job, out of the vast array of pos-sibilities. Perversely, the idea that Ana's life would be shorter than my own gave me an out: I didn't have to choose for a whole lifetime, the way other people did. I could live out this one life as far as it would take me, and then, after it ended, I could go live some other life.

Now there is another shift within me; my internal landscape has changed. For one thing, I feel more physically vulnerable myself; I'm no longer sure that I myself will live to be fifty, much less seventy or eighty. I *may;* it's probable that I will; but I can't count on it. *No guarantees.* And now it seems that Ana may live much longer than we'd thought. *We really may spend our lives together,* I think now. *How do I feel about that?*

And this change is still too new for me to answer that question directly, but it's not hard to identify what I *don't* feel: the old tugging discontent, the longing to escape. I have planted myself deeply here.

⊰≈⊱

One of my favorite summer activities is picking blackberries. No matter where I've lived, no matter how urban the place, I've always managed to find the secret bushes, the cache of free, untamed city fruit.

I like to go just before dusk, when it's not too hot and, if the fog hasn't yet rolled in from the city, not too cold. These days my favorite patch is on Redwood Road, right near some riding stables; as I pick I listen to the horses running, thumping around their track. It's infinitely relaxing. The air is still. It's a kind of moving meditation, my mind able to wander, to let go of its usual chatter, as I search out and reach for the ripe berries.

Tonight as I pick and eat and fill my plastic container, I think about my decision to give a kidney to Ana. When people have asked me about it, I've mostly said it never really felt like a choice. I'm no ace at self-sacrifice; I'm so squeamish it's hard for me even to give blood. But the woman I loved and lived with was sick and in pain, unable to think clearly, to bathe or eat. Donating a kidney to Ana seemed like the quickest way to make our lives better—not just her life, but mine as well.

The real decision, of course, had come much earlier. Once I'd decided I wanted to be with Ana, the rest unfolded day by day, not by choice so much as by necessity. Since no one in Ana's family could give her a kidney, if I hadn't been willing to donate—or if we hadn't shared a blood type, Type A, which is common to forty percent of the population—she would have faced the kidney waiting list. At the time we looked into it, the average wait for a type-A kidney was eighteen months, although of course there were no guarantees, and some people wait much longer.

People do make it through that wait, of course. But Ana was miserable on dialysis, and I was miserable along with her. It seemed to me that giving her my kidney would provide a way out of purgatory for us both.

During the months of tests, all through the endless delays, I was eager to do it. Once the doctors finally cleared me, though, and we scheduled the surgery for ten days later, I panicked. I worried about unlikely things: dying on the operating table, permanent paralysis from the anesthesia. And I feared for my own future, a future that no one could guarantee, no matter how good the statistics for kidney donors were. What if my remaining kidney got damaged? What if living with one kidney somehow cut years off my life?

Of course, I didn't talk to Ana about these fears.

Friends raised other types of concerns. If I gave Ana a kidney, would it change the dynamic in our relationship? they asked. Might Ana feel forever indebted to me, in a way which would render us less than equal partners? Would I feel afterward that she owed me something?

But these questions didn't worry Ana at all, and because they didn't, because her understanding of our motives was so pure and clear, they didn't worry me either. Ana told me that if our situations were reversed, she would donate a kidney to me without a moment's hesitation, and I knew this was true. For Ana, love wasn't something to be tallied up under the headings of "yours" and "mine"; her sense of it was far broader, more sweeping. When we were first dating, the things she said during sex were strange to me, compelling and alarming—"*Mía*," she'd say with her hands on her body, *mine*; "*Tuya, tuya*," she told me when I touched her. *Yours.* It was new to me, how fiercely she wanted to surrender herself to me, how completely she insisted on taking me. She loved the way her culture had taught her, with a consuming loyalty and generosity; to her way of thinking it was natural that I would give her one of my vital organs, simply because I could, because she needed it.

Once we knew for sure that I was cleared to be her donor, I got on the phone. I'd heard through the transplant grapevine about some exciting research going on at the University of California, San Francisco, just up the hill from the transplant center we'd been using. Doctors at UCSF were working to induce a state they called *chimerism*, a kind of truce between the immune systems of donor and recipient. They began by transplanting specially-treated bone marrow cells from the prospective organ donor, trying to induce the recipient's immune system to accept these cells without rejection. If it worked, they reasoned, then perhaps an organ transplant from the same donor could be performed—without the recipient having to remain on immunosuppressive drugs forever after.

It was astonishingly easy to set up a meeting with one of the doctors in charge. There wasn't an official study going on, the work was too new; but patients who were insistent enough were getting involved nonetheless.

Dr. Samuels was young and slight, boyish in his enthusiasm. He was also candid. They'd done the procedure with rats and mice, he said, and it had worked. But they'd only tried it on three people so far, all of whom had had—and lost—previously transplanted kidneys. This was a tough sample group, as their immune systems were already primed for rejection, but they were also the patients who had the least to lose; even another conventional transplant wouldn't offer them great odds. On the first two people, it hadn't worked; their bodies had rallied so hard against the donor kidneys that they'd had to be removed. After that, though, the doctors had changed their technique, and so far it looked as though the third try might be a success—though it was really too soon to know, as the transplant had taken place only two months before.

If we were interested, Dr. Samuels said, they would remove some of my bone marrow, treat it to remove the cells most likely to trigger rejection, then inject it into Ana. Then we would have to wait three months, to see how her body reacted. If she had a strong immune response against my bone marrow cells, I would become ineligible to give her a kidney. If, on the other hand, the bone marrow "took," the kidney transplant could proceed, with less immunosuppression than normal, and with the hope of getting off the medications entirely somewhere down the line.

To me, it seemed a hard call. The possible results were thrilling, yet the risk was high, and the research was terribly new. I waited for Ana's response.

She didn't waver. "Thank you for explaining all this to us," she told the doctor graciously, "but I'm not interested." It wasn't the risk, the uncertainty which bothered her, she told me later; it was the idea of an extra three months on dialysis. That felt unthinkable to her, no matter what the later payback might be.

Afterward we drove out to the ocean. It had been months since we'd been there together, and the beach looked uncommonly beautiful. Sun glittered over everything; the endless gray-green waves swelled large and broke, swelled large and broke, turning themselves to thick white rushing foam, then flattening into vast sweeps of sea-water again. I kissed Ana's forehead, trying to imagine a future for us. It seemed to me then that even if there *were* no future, even if the transplant failed, my lips on her skin would be indelible. Nothing could take them away.

⌘

Then there were other phone calls I made. One was to Joseph, a hypnotherapist and guided visualization specialist in Berkeley. I'd never done any such work before, never even contemplated it, but then, I'd also never spent even so much as a single night in a hospital; I'd always winced and looked away when my blood was drawn. Now I was voluntarily agreeing to undergo major surgery, to have one of my vital organs removed, and the panic had hit.

On my first visit, Joseph urged me to identify a healing animal, a safe place, somewhere I could go in my mind for comfort both before and after the operation. He used massage, a sunlamp, a scattering of acupuncture needles to try to relax me, to take me *through* my fear instead of around it. He suggested I try to talk to my kidneys, to the one which would be removed—expressing my gratitude for its courage, saying thank-you and goodbye—and to the one which would remain, thanking it too, and grieving with it for its loss.

These were ideas I was skeptical of, with one part of my mind, and yet I needed them. I feared that my body wouldn't, couldn't forgive me for voluntarily giving up one of my vital organs. I worried that I would never feel fully healthy afterward, that what I had done—however logical to my mind, however spurred by love—would be experienced purely as an assault by my physical self. There was that split: me, and then my body, as if we were two entities; it was me who'd made the decision, but it was my body which would pay for it.

Joseph listened calmly as I poured all this out, and though I half-hoped he would ask me if I was sure I wanted to go through with the transplant, he didn't. His belief in my commitment was unwavering. On my second visit to him, after trying unsuccessfully to make contact with a "healing animal"—I tried to imagine my fat half-Siamese cat in the role, but she seemed too self-centered to fit the bill—I found myself remembering a tree I'd climbed once at Point Reyes, a huge crook of branches where I'd sat for hours, looking out over a golden field. "Good, good," Joseph said. "That's a place you can return to, when you need to. You can leave your body there for safekeeping when you go into surgery, and go back to claim it later."

I sniffled, still a little dubious, then blew my nose and wiped my eyes. The transplant was four days away.

The weekend before, I'd taken Ana with me to see another alternative-therapy practitioner, a woman named Colleen who lived in Sausalito and did something called Neurolinguistic Programming, or NLP. This was a technique which seemed deceptively simple, yet, according to its followers, had the potential to bring about deep change by speaking directly to the unconscious mind. I'd heard that NLP was successful with allergies, which practitioners considered "phobias of the immune system"; that gave me the idea that maybe, by speaking directly to Ana's immune system, we could keep it from rejecting the kidney. I said as much to Colleen, who promptly corrected me.

"Don't think in terms of her immune system *not rejecting* the kidney. That's negative language. When you talk like that, the body might fail to hear the word *not* and pick up on the word *rejection* instead. You have to tell her body to *accept* the kidney, to welcome it."

All right then, that was what we would do. Colleen placed pieces of paper on her rug to serve as stepping stones; on each step of the path we were to talk about what we hoped for from the transplant, which Colleen called "this journey." By naming our hopes about this journey, she told us, we could make them reality. If we needed to say something about a fear, we would have to step off the path to do it, so as not to muddy our trail with the negative.

Step One. Ana and I balanced awkwardly together on the first piece of paper.

"I want us to get through the surgery with little pain . . ." I began.

"No, no, no," Colleen admonished me. "You're still talking in the negative. Say, 'I want us to get through the surgery in comfort.'"

"Okay. I want us to get through the surgery in comfort. I want us to heal quickly and—" I stopped myself before I said the words I was thinking, *no complications*. "To heal quickly, and to have the course of our healing be smooth."

"I want my body to welcome Ruth's kidney," Ana said. "To see it as a friend, a helper, not—" She paused, stopping herself from saying the words which had come first to her mind: *not as an intruder*. "To see it as a friend."

We moved together onto the second piece of paper. "I want us to be happy and healthy, together and separately," I said. "I want our relationship to continue to grow."

"I want our love to grow stronger through this experience," Ana continued.

On the third piece of paper, I said, "I want us to have a passionate sexual relationship again, after the transplant."

"I want us to be equal partners in life, *for* life," Ana chimed in.

And so we continued on the paper path, naming our hopes and desires. It felt kind of hokey to me, but Ana looked intent, focused on each step.

When we reached the last piece of paper Colleen told us that we could embrace, and we did, almost as if this were a wedding; we kissed and I pulled Ana's body close, losing myself in her for a moment, not even caring that we were in the white-on-white living room of some woman we didn't know.

After we pulled apart again Ana said, "It wasn't only you I was hugging."

"What do you mean?"

"There was a hawk following above me, while we were doing the different steps. On the last step, he came down, and his body was as big as a person's. He was hugging me, dancing with me."

"I saw it too," Colleen said. "It gave me goose-bumps."

So I'm the only one who didn't see this human-sized hawk. I shrug helplessly.

"It will go well," Colleen told us. "Your surgery will go well."

And that was Ana's first contact with her *gavilán*.

I remember all this while I pick blackberries, and it feels like a lifetime ago. How blindly I reached out then, in my fear; how far afield I traveled from my usual sources of strength, my writing, my friends, my logical mind—my familiar sense of the world.

But the day after the surgery, when my spinal block anesthesia wore off and the pain seemed to root me to my hospital bed, I had visited the tree Joseph helped me find. I saw myself climbing into its crook, finding my naked body there, and holding it in my arms as it sobbed. When it was finally done crying, I carried it down with me, through the field to an apple orchard, and there, beneath one of the apple trees, we found Ana lying on a gurney. *There*, I said to my body, *that's why we did this*. And my body seemed to understand, and covered Ana with grateful, tearful kisses. I cried too, alone in my hospital bed, and finally slept. The next day, I awoke without pain.

Ana's *gavilán* has remained a strong presence in her life since then. And some of the wishes we named in Colleen's living room have already come to pass.

We are moving forward.

❧

One weekend in August we go to a North Berkeley street fair, blocks and blocks of music, artists, clowns. There's a fantastically decorated Volkswagen Bug on display, its entire frame a mosaic of glued bits of glass and marbles; a sign says it took fourteen years to make. There's a 1960s-style band on another corner, decked out in bellbottoms and suede fringe, strumming "A Hard Day's Night."

The smell of food is everywhere: skewers of barbecuing beef, vats of chow mein, great hunks of sausage slabs on fresh-baked bread. Ana and I walk and walk. We're going uphill slightly; she doesn't seem to mind. The sun is hot on my bare shoulders. I feel chic and cool in my sundress and two-dollar straw hat.

"A few months ago the smell of all this food would've made you sick," I say. "You wouldn't have been able to walk all these blocks. Not even half of *one* block."

"No," Ana agrees, firm and solid and alive beside me now.

It's one of those epiphany moments for me, like the one I had a year and a half ago at my friend Jean-Paul's place in Santa Cruz. I'd stood on his little balcony, looking out at the ocean, while the sad sweet longing soundtrack from the movie "The Piano" drifted around me. Ana came and stood behind me, and I leaned back into her arms. *My dying lover,* I thought. *And Jean-Paul, my dying friend.* I'd known for six years that Jean-Paul was HIV-positive; now he'd had an outbreak of shingles. His health couldn't last forever, it seemed. *But we are all dying,* I thought then, *only some of us a little more quickly.* I turned, moving my eyes through his studio cottage: the white curtains' edges licked up by the breeze, the blown-glass vase of calla lilies on the table, the bright angles of sunlight on the polished tile floor, and Jean-Paul himself, in the kitchen, warming milk for *café au lait.* It was a moment infinitely sweet, infinitely sad.

So now there is this other kind of epiphany; the music has changed to a danceable rhythm. The last time I talked to Jean-Paul, he had great news: his T-cell count had actually risen, after years of remaining stable at a fairly low level; now it's edged itself just barely into the normal range. Ana walks along beside me now, my kidney filtering her blood. *We are all still dying,* I think. But right now it doesn't feel that way. There's been a shift, as subtle yet far-reaching as the shifting of tectonic plates that brings the earth closer to, or further from, its own destruction. We're having fun again.

❧

Ana gets a letter from her HMO which we read together on the bed:

Dear Ms. Rodriguez,
Our records indicate that you are diabetic. We recommend a yearly test for microalbumin in the urine, as there are new treatments available for

diabetic kidney disease if it is caught early. Please contact your primary care physician to schedule this test.

"Don't their records also indicate that you had a kidney transplant four months ago?" I ask, gasping through teary laughter.

"Guess not," Ana shrugs.

SIX

Four months after the transplant, summer's long days are disappearing fast. One evening in September I get home at 7:30, the sky a deep twilight already, that rich midnight blue that will soon be black. As always, the dogs greet me at the door, yipping and jumping, their nails clicking like castanets on the wood floor; somehow, though, the rest of the house seems strangely silent. Then Ana's voice comes down the stairs in a weak-sounding croak. "Up here."

She's lying on the bed, her face slack. She's been in pain since 5:30, she says. It started in her back, radiated around to her abdomen. It's bad; her face contorts.

"Why didn't you call me?" I demand.

"I didn't want to panic. I kept thinking it would go away." She gestures feebly toward the digital thermometer on her bedside table. "I took my temp, but I didn't even look at it."

I check the thermometer. 98.6° exactly.

"Have you called the doctor?"

"No, I was waiting for you to get home."

The pain seems to be getting worse; she's pale, grimacing, clenching at the quilt. Outside the evening has turned cool, but the bedroom, which bakes in sun all afternoon, is stuffy and hot; Ana's skin feels clammy to the touch. Is she just sweaty, or is it something else? "My sugar's fifty-nine," she adds weakly. "I ate dinner, but it feels like it didn't go down."

I run downstairs for some juice for her, then call the transplant center, do battle with the languid answering-service operator. "When was the transplant?" she queries. "How do you spell Rodriguez? Does that end with an *s* or a *z*?" The doctor on call will get back to us, she says finally, hanging up.

But now I don't think we can wait. Ana's in too much pain.

"Come on. I'm going to take you to the hospital."

"But I can't get dressed."

"I'll help you."

"But the doctor hasn't called back yet."

"We can call him again from the car phone." I guide each of her legs into a pair of sweatpants, her feet into the big fleecy slippers I bought her for her birthday three years ago.

"I feel like I'm gonna throw up."

"That's okay. I'll bring a bag."

I extract her insurance card from her wallet and slip it into my pocket, help her down the stairs. The dogs dance briefly around our legs again, puzzled but hopeful. If she felt better Ana would speak "for" them, as she usually does, high-pitching her voice: "What's happening? *A dónde van?* Can we come too?"

But tonight we leave so quickly, so quietly, as if we've been transported into some sped-up silent movie. I'm on autopilot again, smooth and calm, careening us down the dark road at 75, 80, 85. I keep my hands steady on the wheel, shift my gaze quickly back and forth between the highway and Ana's face. The pain seems to come in waves; her body slumps into tolerance for a few minutes, then clenches tight again as the cramping intensifies.

The night is clear, white-eyed with oncoming headlights; not a lot of traffic going into the city at this hour. My mind goes fast and steady as the car. *No fever; it's not an infection, then. But the doctors said before that with her immune system so suppressed, her body might not spike a fever even if she did have an infection—so maybe that can't be ruled out. Sudden onset—would lymphoma show up like that? Doesn't seem likely. So maybe it's an infection after all. Maybe* CMV. Cytomegalovirus isn't a problem for healthy people; at least half the U.S. population carries it, and I know *I* do. They wrote it right on Ana's transplant chart: donor CMV+. *Generally asymptomatic in the immunocompetent, but potentially fatal in the immunosuppressed; commonly flares up 3–6 months post-transplant; treated with* IV *ganciclovir, which has dramatically reduced the mortality rate.* My memory clicks through textbook facts. I don't have the skills or knowledge to diagnose Ana, but I imagine that I do.

But what if it *is* lymphoma? *Four months post-transplant,* I remember the medical book had said. *Aggressive, widely disseminated.* Smoothly, dispassionately, I race us down the freeway, still scanning from Ana's face to the dark road and back again. *It will still have been worth it,* I think, *for this time we've had.* A few days ago, on Sunday morning, we'd made love; Ana's touch had melted me. I exhaled in her arms and felt myself go limp, surrendering to her hands, her grip. Lips on my neck. Teeth on my nipples. Nails rasping against my belly. Fingers deep inside me. And I was able to make love to her, too, and it was nothing like the old days, but something nonetheless; with my tongue I felt her moisten and swell, her body moving feebly toward the old rhythms. Then we went out to a waterslide park, floated together on giant inner tubes down an artificial river. We linked hands with two friends, the four of us bobbing and spinning and laughing in the sunny water. *It will all have been worth it. If she dies now, it will have been enough.*

We speak our love so often. "*Te quiero mucho,*" I told her sleepily this morning, when she got out of bed at 6:00 A.M. If she dies now, I will not mourn things unsaid. Even the trips we've wanted to take together, and haven't yet—New Mexico, Guatemala, Greece, Brazil—we've talked of them so often, read through so many guidebooks together, it's almost as it would have been if we had gone.

We're over the bridge now and in the city, these streets so familiar, so laden with memories for us both. "We're almost there," I tell Ana, my hand on her thigh; but she's not here, she's deep into the valley of her pain.

Inside the E.R. the triage nurse ushers us quickly into a room; half a room, really, partitioned by curtains. On the other side of the curtain a skinny young red-haired woman seems to be holding court. Ana lies on the table, moaning, while we wait for the nurse to come back with her tools, blood-pressure cuff and glucometer, tubes and syringe to draw blood; but above and below her moans I can hear the red-haired woman cooing at the people around her—are they nurses? doctors? Why are there so many people in the room? "I'm on Zoloft," she tells them. "What was that prescribed for?" a male voice asks. "Major depression." "How long have you been on it?" "About a year." Her voice is delicate with regret. "And do you know the reason for your depression?" Now the red-haired woman laughs, a fluttery, practiced laugh. "If I knew the reason . . . " she begins. "Well, it's complicated. I've been in therapy for years . . . "

It seems to take Ana's nurse a very long time to line up her supplies; she keeps thinking of something else she needs, then disappearing back into the hospital labyrinth to look for it. Even once she's got everything there she moves so much slower than Ana does with these familiar tasks: pricking the finger, squeezing the ruby drop of blood into the little circle on the test strip, swabbing the fingertip with alcohol. Ana's blood sugar is still low, fifty-six this time, but her blood pressure is very high, 213 over 93. "We'll take it again in a few minutes," soothes the nurse. "It's always higher when you're upset." And of course Ana's upset, gasping with the pain in her back, lying down and then sitting up again as the waves of nausea hit.

"I don't like my body," I hear the red-haired woman saying plaintively. A smooth female voice answers her, "You've got a fine body. At least you're not an old lady, like me." "But I don't like my body. I wish I could trade it in for a different one," the redhead says again, waiting coyly, I think, to be reassured, contradicted; and I feel disgusted by her, by her cloying, ordinary, self-indulgent problems. When I first started doing AIDS work I went through a period of fury at any healthy person who attempted suicide; I knew so many people who wanted badly to live, whose lives were being taken from them. The idea of a physically healthy person willfully taking his own life seemed like such a travesty. And what I feel now is similar: the woman I love lies on one side of the curtain, crying out in pain, while a woman on the other side, apparently physically intact, talks about wanting to trade her body in for a new one. I catch the nurse's eye; she shrugs.

Ana's blood tests all come back unremarkable, her white cell count smack in the middle of the normal range—so it really must not be an infection, then. Her creatinine is 1.5, which is great, the best it's been since the transplant; that rules out a rejection episode. The transplant nephrologist on call finally arrives; it's Dr. Lucca, the same doctor who managed Ana immediately after the transplant. The one who encouraged her to take fish oil. The one who put her on Procardia.

"Have you ever had stones in your native kidneys? Gallstones? Ulcers?" he queries now. No. No. No. "I don't know what it is," he says finally, "but I'm going to admit you. We'll run some tests tomorrow, abdominal CT scan, maybe an upper endoscopy, see if we can't check it out." He gives her a shot of morphine, and we wait for her pain to lessen, for her to be wheeled upstairs to the ward we know so well.

And the next day Ana goes through all the promised tests: the scan, x-rays, even the upper endoscopy, where a doctor sticks a scope down through her mouth to her esophagus and takes a look around. They find nothing remarkable, though just for the hell of it they take a sample of a pink-looking area in her esophagus. Overnight and through the next day Ana's pain gradually lessens, then finally disappears on its own. They'll keep her one more day while they wait for the biopsy results from the pink spot, but they don't expect it to be anything.

Driving home from the hospital that night, soothed now into believing that Ana will be fine after all, I drift back into travel fantasies. I imagine us at the Saturday market in Chichicastenango, on the black sand beach whose name I don't remember, squeezing onto the buses filled with people and chickens and goats; and yet it was only last night—last night! less than twenty-four hours ago—that I imagined her dead.

I remember a night years ago, one of the times Jean-Paul and I stayed up drinking tea in his kitchen until after midnight, in the early days of our friendship, when so much less was known about HIV; both he and I assumed then that he'd be dead within a few years. He and his lover were planning a trip to France, but he'd get a ticket with an open return date, he told me, just in case; and he hoped to be able to take the trip, but he accepted the idea that perhaps he wouldn't. He was planning for both possibilities at once. At the time his attitude seemed very wise to me, yet also inordinately sad. Yet now I've learned to do that, too, I realize with surprise. I've learned to live both ways at once, as if Ana's life will be long, and as if she may die at any time.

❧

"Gallbladder attack," says a co-worker knowledgeably when I describe Ana's symptoms to her the next day.

"But they checked for gallstones. They didn't find any."

"Doesn't matter; that kind of pain comes from the gallbladder. It happens to me too, if I eat too much fatty food. It comes on just the way you said—starting in the back, radiating to the front. Nausea, too. There's nothing to do for it but take pain pills and wait for it to pass—and try to avoid fatty foods in the future," she counsels.

The doctor hadn't said anything of the kind. "We don't know," he'd said, after a few thousand dollars' worth of invasive tests, and two nights in the hospital. But what my co-worker said makes sense to me—more sense, anyway, than accepting that there's no explanation.

❧

A week or so later, on a gorgeous sunny fall Saturday, we wake up early for no reason at all and decide to drive down the coast. On the last long uphill stretch before the road winds down to the huge, sparkling expanse of ocean, I ask Ana suddenly, "Do you still feel worried about the kidney failing?"

"I don't think about it," she says. "I try to live day to day, enjoying what I have right now. But," she adds thoughtfully, "I did find myself thinking the other day, it'll be nice in a few more years when I've got my car paid off. I'll have more spending money."

"So you were thinking about the future. Expecting it to happen."

She nods.

"Is that different from how it used to be?"

"Oh, *sí*. When I was so sick before the transplant, I couldn't think of the future at all. I just focused on making it through each day."

"You couldn't really imagine that you'd ever feel better," I surmise.

"No," she agrees.

The autumn crispness of the day reminds me of the day eleven months ago, Halloween, in fact, when we first visited the transplant center for Ana's pre-transplant evaluation.

"I remember when the nurse asked you if you were nauseous and throwing up in the mornings *yet*, and we thought, So that's what's coming," I say. "At that time you didn't seem *that* sick to me, but I remember asking whether after the transplant your quality of life would be better than it was at that point, and being so relieved when the answer was yes. You do feel better now than you did a year ago, don't you?"

"Oh, yes," Ana says. "No comparison. I was already dragging myself through each day then."

"And you're not, now?" I search her face for confirmation.

"No," she laughs. "Now I feel fine, *gracias a* Rinita." Rina is the name she's given to my kidney, derived from the Spanish word *riñón*; sometimes, as now, she uses the affectionate diminutive Rinita.

"I met someone at the conference yesterday who's had her kidney for ten years, and it's still working fine," I tell her. I'd gone to a seminar held by the National Kidney Foundation, heard projections for transplantation years into the future. Some of the more exotic possibilities involved xenotransplantation, using organs from pigs or other animals, or growing whole new kidneys from fetal kidney stem cells, which, when injected into the blood of rabbits with failing kidneys, traveled directly to the working nephrons and began to construct a new, functional organ around them. Of course, none of this research had any real relevance for us. "And I saw Liz; she's had hers for seven or eight years, and it's fine, too. I'm starting to feel more confident," I tell her. "There really are lots of people around who do fine for years and years. It seems like there's a good chance you'll be one of them."

It's hard to remember, now, why I felt so frightened a few months ago; but then, I'm good at this kind of forgetting. The minute the rains end and the sun comes out, it's just as if it's always been that way. Ana's process is different, I know; she's much slower to heal, and, as she's said about the scar on her belly, she heals "from the inside out."

❦

At October's support group meeting we spend most of our time talking about the people waiting for livers. Sarah is in the ICU; she's been there for over a week, frailer than ever, with nothing to do but hope an organ will come in time. "She's gained a couple new tubes though," says Erich, who still seems calm, even cheerful, though we learn later that he's been put on leave from his job; he was getting "too angry," his boss said.

Sarah's had her T-tube for months now; it funnels the bile that her liver is no longer able to push into her bile duct, but the tube entry and exit sites keep getting infected. So last week, "while they had her in there and they didn't have anything else to do," Erich says, the doctors decided to remove her old T-tube and replace it with two smaller ones. Unfortunately, in the process they spread the infection throughout her body; she wound up with septicemia and had to be on IV antibiotics for several days. "The worst part of it is," Erich lowers his voice, "that on the day they discovered the infection, they had a liver for her. They would've transplanted her!"

"But they couldn't? Because of the infection?" someone asks.

"That's right. She doesn't know that yet. Won't ever know it, unless I tell her. I only know it because a couple of days later I went to the support group they hold there at the hospital, and there was a guy in there who'd just gotten a liver. 'Yeah, there was someone worse off than me that was gonna get it, but at the last minute she couldn't, so I lucked out,' he said. No shit, Sherlock, he lucked out!"

You'd have to know this man well to be able to distinguish between calm and anguish in his tone, I realize. Too often they've sounded the same to me, just as in my early days with Ana, the first time I took her to the hospital, the sounds of pain and fear she made seemed much like her sounds of pleasure when we made love. I have a sense of Erich's pain from the fact that he's been put on leave from work; but if I didn't know, his face and voice would never tell me.

"We almost lost her last week," Erich adds. "But she's doing better now. At least she responded to the antibiotics; the infection's better. So it's back to the waiting game."

Gene is here without Dorey tonight, and he reports on the research they've done. Most of Northern California is designated as one region in terms of liver allocation, and in this region there are currently 659 people on the waiting list. "I calculated that at the rate they're doing transplants now, my turn wouldn't come up for at least two years—either that or until I get as bad as Sarah," he grimaces. "But it turns out that the Sacramento area has designated its own region. UC Davis is up there; they just started doing transplants. They've only done about ten so far; they're not certified yet, but I called them up and they were real friendly. And get this—for blood type A there are only *ten people* on the waiting list!"

"That's amazing," we murmur.

"And I can be on both waiting lists at once. You know how everyone said Mickey Mantle got his liver legitimately, without jumping the waiting list? Well, that's true, he didn't jump any *one* list; he just went around and got on every separate waiting list in the country. Spent about a hundred thousand bucks doing it. Me, I don't have that kind of money," Gene adds, and we all laugh. "But hey, I figure Sacramento's a good bet. They've got a couple million people in the metropolitan area, and it's a young, healthy population; must be a lot of drunk driving, right? I've got two bumper stickers on my car now: there's the one with the green recycling symbol, *Recycle Yourself: Be an Eye, Organ and Tissue Donor,* most of you've got that one, and then right next to it I've got *Repeal the Helmet Laws.*" More laughter from the group.

Gene's a survivor, I think, and Dorey's a veritable whirlwind of organization. He hands out a newsletter she's printed up, listing all the fundraising events they're holding so they can pay their share of expenses when the time comes.

Ana proudly tells everyone how she managed to get her Prednisone dose reduced. At her last visit the doctor had put her on an alternating schedule, 15 mg. one day, 20 the next; that was to ease her down from the daily 20 mg. dose she'd been on for the preceding month. But the high-low schedule wreaked havoc with her appetite, her blood sugar, her moods, so I encouraged her to call the clinic back. "The nurse coordinator said, 'Oh no, I wouldn't advise you to go down to just 15 mg. a day; this is how we do it, we can't take any chances with that kidney,' and I said, 'Could you just please go and *ask* the doctor for me?" And five minutes later she called me back to say the doctor said it was fine," Ana reports, triumphant.

Most of the support group members feel the same way; of course no one wants to "take any chances," but everyone wants to be on the lowest workable doses of meds, to ease the side effects. It's easy enough for the docs to write a prescription, but they don't have to live with the results.

"I'm so proud of you," I'd told Ana the day she told me about getting the Prednisone lowered. "You've learned how to be your own advocate, and I know it hasn't come easily for you."

"In Puerto Rico people think doctors are like gods," she'd said. "You don't question what they tell you; you just do it."

The next struggle was getting Ana's gynecologist to agree to test her hormone levels, because her periods are shorter than they used to be, and her libido is still low. When Ana first asked, back in July, the gynecologist told her there was no point, because "your hormones are bound to be out of whack anyway, with all the medications you're on." "That's not good enough!" I'd wailed when Ana repeated it back to me. "We want to know *what's* out of whack, how it affects you, what can be done about it." But it took us almost three months to approach the gynecologist again. Finally Ana asked me to talk to her, and I put a call in, but when she called back I wasn't home, and Ana screwed up her courage and talked to her. "The nephrologist said there's no reason for my hormones to be out of balance at this stage," she told her. "He *suggested* I get my hormones checked." This was, essentially, true, although of course we'd been the ones to bring it up to the nephrologist. The gynecologist bought it, and agreed. Score two for Ana!

But when the hormone tests come back, we're frustrated again. After all that wrangling we'd thought the gynecologist would order a full panel, but instead she just checked Ana's estrogen level, nothing more. "It's fine," she assures Ana. "Nowhere near menopause." So there's still no explanation for the short periods, the sore breasts, the vanished sex drive. *Another gynecologist*, we say to each other. *A second opinion*. Or maybe an endocrinologist would be the next step? But with so many doctors' appointments to coordinate, it's hard to take on yet another.

❧

Five months.

We wake together, lie there sleepily stroking each other, and then before I've even begun to wonder whether we'll make love, whether she'll want to, whether I will, whether it will work or just turn into another painful disappointment, Ana's mouth is on my breast; her hands arc around to the small of my back, cupping me to her, and I feel my whole being exhale, opening to her touch.

Then when I roll her onto her back I graze her chest with my lips and breasts, move my mouth over her belly, reddish-purple with scars, the long gash where they cut her to put my kidney inside, the two smaller welts where the peritoneal dialysis catheter entered and left her body, and an array of yellowish-blue bruises from her four daily insulin shots. I kiss her everywhere here, all this lush, rippled, creamy, long-suffering flesh, then move down with my hands to stroke her inner thighs, the mound of pubis; by the time I put my tongue to her there she's arching her body up toward me, lifting her thighs so I can reach her better, and I burrow deeper and deeper into her, my own body shaking with her desire.

Afterward we shower together, loudly singing Spanish love songs: *Yo sé que eres tú . . . la que yo tanto he esperado,* and *Quiero que me hagas el amor . . .* I hug her beneath the water's hot stream, breathing in the scent of her kiwi-grapefruit shampoo, watching her breasts move as she lathers her hair.

They are flushed pink, her breasts, networked with tiny broken capillaries—must be another drug side-effect—and I kiss them and think, *I have earned every second of this happiness, every second of it.*

Even happiness is different now; it's different to arrive at a moment like this after a long journey, rather than find ourselves blessed by sweetness after no effort at all. Yet sometimes I still struggle with how badly I crave the sweet moments, the ones as perfect as movie stills: sun dappling the hillside, a checkered picnic blanket spread with bread and cheese and wine, violin music soaring in the background. In real life Ana would never sprawl out on a blanket on the ground; it would be too hard for her to get up afterward, so we'd have to sit at a picnic table instead. And she doesn't drink wine; and there would probably be bugs; and one of us would be looking for a bathroom; and the day would be too hot or too cold; and we'd be missing something, maybe a knife to cut the cheese. Our lives are perfect just as they are—I know this from my readings of Buddhist thought—and perfection rarely comes packaged the way we're expecting it to.

So we go out to our favorite Berkeley breakfast place, my body still limp from our lovemaking, the blood running sweetly slow and thick in my veins; and the restaurant is jarring to me in this state, so much noisier than I remember it—has it always been this loud? And Ana stops in the bathroom on the way out, and stays in there a long time, and when I go knock on the door to check on her she whispers urgently for me to get the latex glove and lubricant from the car. Her bowels have mostly been better lately but sometimes they still act up, and this seems to be one of those times; she's going to have to disimpact herself again.

I used to be so private, so squeamish about bathroom matters; for at least our first year together I couldn't use the toilet with Ana in the room, or even with her in the next room if the door was open. How could someone want to make love to me after they'd seen and heard me pissing and shitting? It seemed to me that being intimately familiar with your lover's more ignoble bodily functions would take away your ability to experience the body in that other way, as the repository of desire and magic. And yet as the years have gone by and I've cleaned up Ana's vomit and diarrhea, watched her disimpact herself, even disimpacted her myself when she was too sick to do it, I've found that my physical desire for her has changed not at all; this passion is fueled by a magic much deeper than those surface tricks. No white rabbit emerging from a hat, no penny pulled from behind an ear—this is a whole love, I tell myself, fuller, richer because of *all* the moments, those that are messy or painful or frustrating, agonizing or banal, as well as those that are blissful or revelatory. And for the most part, I believe this, although sometimes the old disappointment sears through me when things are not as I wish them to be.

Sometimes I argue this point with my friend Kate, whose life tells a different kind of love story. Though married, Kate has for years sustained a very passionate extramarital affair. She and her lover, also married, believe theirs is the best of all possible worlds; they've relegated all the mundane moments, all the struggle and disappointment, to their unsuspecting spouses, so their time with each other is always special, always "quality time." I listen to her and ask, "But don't you miss spending nights together, cuddling in the morning when you wake up? And tender little moments together in the kitchen, and making each other soup when you're sick, and just sitting and reading together in bed at night?"—and yet still a part of me aches with jealousy as Kate describes her storybook romance.

One way or another, you choose, I think. You choose to go for everything, or not, and this everything I've chosen happens to have this particular struggle bundled into it; but still I believe, I've got to believe, that there's a large measure of reward built into it too. I've wondered sometimes, *How would Ana and I live if she didn't have a life-threatening condition? What would we worry and fight about, muddle through, dream of? What would make our lives difficult?*—because undoubtedly something would, something always does; it's just that I can't imagine what it would possibly be. Which is, in itself, a kind of reward; so many of the usual, petty concerns don't even seem to exist for us. Sometimes I don't know whether to laugh or cry at the image of marriage I glean from Ann Landers' column: *Dear Ann, My marriage is falling apart because my husband has grown a beard.* Or, *My wife has gained twenty pounds.* Or, *My husband always leaves his dirty underwear on the bathroom floor.* Or, *My wife spends too much time on the phone*—yes, concerns of an entirely different order of magnitude.

When we get home there is a message on our answering machine. Sarah got her liver.

❦

"My first client today was a seventy-two-year-old man, very well-dressed, well put together," Ana tells me one night over dinner.

"Latino?" I ask. Since Ana's the only bilingual probation officer on the drunk-driving caseload, most of her clients are.

"No, Anglo. Anyway, I said to him, 'I understand you got into an accident while driving intoxicated?' and he said, 'No, it wasn't an accident. I was trying to kill myself.' So without even thinking I said to him, 'That's interesting. You're trying to kill yourself, and I'm trying to stay alive. I had a kidney transplant five months ago, and I take more pills every day than you've ever seen.'"

"What'd he say?"

"He started crying, and then I started crying, too. I told him, 'I tried to kill myself too, when I was sixteen years old, and I thank God every day that I didn't succeed. Life can be so beautiful.' So we sat there and cried together, and then I told him how to fulfill his conditions of probation, and when he left he said 'Can I call you sometime, just to talk? You've helped me so much, I want to be like you; I want to love life the way you do,' and I told him he could call me anytime.

"My next client was a Salvadorean man. I told him, 'I've got good news and bad news. The good news is that if you work with me, we can keep you out of jail. The bad news is that you owe a large amount of restitution, but you can make monthly payments during your two years on probation, and if necessary I can extend your probation for another two years after that.

"He looked at me and said, 'Okay, let's talk money.' So I told him he owes four thousand dollars, plus an additional eighteen hundred in fines and court costs. Then he told me he's been in this country for twenty-three years; his wife and children are back in El Salvador, he's supported them all this time. The night he got arrested he'd found out that his wife was going to have to have surgery, and he was upset because he couldn't be with her. He told me, 'My brother's a minister. My wife is very involved with the church. No one in the family drinks; I'm the black sheep. I've been here so many years, and now I've broken one of this country's laws.' So I told him, *'No sea tan duro con usted mismo*, don't be so hard on yourself. You made a mistake, but you can set it right; I'm here to help you do that.' So he left saying, 'I'll do it, Niña Ana'—*asi hablan los Salvadoreños*, that's how the Salvadoreans talk. He's a mechanic, but he doesn't have a shop; he just works on cars in the street. Do you know what it's like for someone like that to try to come up with two hundred dollars a month? *Pero el hombre se fue más contento que un niño*, he was pleased as punch when he left, even though I'd just told him he owes almost six thousand dollars!"

"*Tu me inspiras*," I tell Ana, and it's true, she inspires me; she takes a role most people see as punitive and uses it to better peoples' lives. Ana chuckles, "After I got done talking with the first guy, one of the new P.O.s, Hugo, he could see I'd been crying, he asked me all concerned, 'What's wrong? Are you all right?' I told him, 'I'm fine; I was just sharing in some of the pain and anguish of one of my clients.' He looked at me like he couldn't believe what he was hearing. 'Isn't that what we're here for, to share with our clients, to try to help them?' I said. *Se quedó* speechless."

"What do you think has changed?" I ask her. "I mean, you've always tried to help people."

"Yes, but now I have more compassion. I'm more ready to say, 'Who am I to judge?' Because of all the pain I've gone through, I think, 'Maybe this person has also gone through pain, physical, emotional.'

"And your love makes it possible for me to do this," Ana tells me. "Your love makes a balance in my life. I see so many bitter people at work; they don't have anyone who loves them the way you love me."

Now there are tears in my eyes too. "You're a strong person," I say, "but still, when I try to imagine you, anyone, going through this last year alone . . ."

"I couldn't have done it," Ana says simply. And I press my wet cheek to hers, feeling how right she is: how none of us exists alone in this world, and how, by really loving just one other person, we touch so many other people's lives.

⊱⊰

Down the block from us, a woman is dying. I've never met her, but I know her house; I've often thought of her as I passed it, wondering how she was.

Months ago, she called the cancer hotline where I work now to get information about her breast cancer, which had been diagnosed late. She told me the cancer had already spread to the lymph nodes above her collarbone. When she gave me her address, so I could send her some pamphlets, I realized that she was my neighbor; of course, because our service is confidential, I said nothing. But I remembered her.

Today Luther, who also lives down the street, who does odd jobs for all of us in the neighborhood when he's not drinking his "brewsky," as he calls it, came by to clean our gutters. Luther knows everyone. He told me the woman with cancer is named Lawanda; she's thirty-seven, exactly halfway between my age and Ana's. She has two children, four-year-old twins.

"How's she doing?" I asked.

He shook his head. "Very sad. The cancer's all up in her brain."

So now when I pass her house, a neat wood-frame building set back from the street, I see it differently. It's the tragedy that could have chosen me and yet, for now, has chosen someone else; it's the cars rolling over and over, then bursting into flame that I saw once in my rearview mirror, having passed the place of the accident just seconds before. The autumn sky is full of crows, huge black shiny arrogant birds I've always loved for the sheer fierceness of their presence; but Luther sees them and says, "Them crows mean death."

SEVEN

Six months.

Six months, and Ana still startles at her bright-red gash of a scar.

Six months, and she's graduated to getting her blood work done only once every two weeks. (At first it was twice weekly, then once per week.) She takes her blood pressure only once a day now, her temperature not at all—"Only if you feel sick," the doctor agreed. There are still the four daily pinpricks for the blood sugar testing, but she's been doing that for years already. Since she went onto the new immunosuppressant, Cellsept, her creatinine hasn't risen above 2.0.

Six months, and we've decided to try again with a pair of kittens. The ones we get this time are bigger, healthier, less needy. There's Cielito Lindo, a feisty little black-and-white boy with tuxedo markings, and Mota, a fuzzy white powder puff of a girl. But we call them by other names too; the two of them together are either *los monstritos*, "the little monsters," or *los enanos*, "the midgets." The boy gets nicknamed Tuxedo-Boy, and Mota becomes La Princesa, because of her poised, regal posture; they race around gaily, attacking Ana's giant snake-plant, our bodies under the covers, anything that moves. Ana teaches Tuxedo-Boy to dance, holding his two front paws up and waltzing him around, singing her own version of "La Bamba":

Para bailar la bamba, se necesita un gatito en tuxedo . . .

"To dance the bamba, you need a little cat in a tuxedo . . ."

We're future-dreaming more and more these days; when we get tired of this hectic Bay Area life we'll move to New Mexico to retire, find ourselves an adobe *casita*, we imagine. We plan a sightseeing trip there, for next summer. We plan, that's the main thing. We plan.

Our transplant support group invites a shaman to the meeting, and he does a ritual in which Ana discovers that her *gavilán* is not, after all, her medicine animal. He's her spirit guide, she explains to me later; her medicine animal is a black panther with piercing green eyes. I nod, envious, dubious. I missed that meeting, so I have no idea what "my" animals are.

"The shaman said each organ has a soul," Ana tells me. I nod. This feels true to me; how else to really explain the fact that my kidney works in Ana's body—that *any* organ, removed from one body, removed from the brain which supposedly directed it, still does its lifesaving work?

Of course, the doctors have an explanation, one that doesn't involve the word *soul* at all. And sometimes I find myself straddling the fence, on one side the part of me that knows that what has happened to us is much larger than Western medicine can ever quantify, and on the other side the part that still reads medical journals like the gospel. Lately I've caught myself telling new acquaintances casually that "Ana needed a kidney transplant, and I ended up being her donor," and afterwards I want to go back and blot out those words. "Ended up"—how slight, how trivial that sounds, and how far it is from the truth of the journey we made and still are making.

The night before Thanksgiving, I find a kitten mewing outside Wal-Mart. He's small, black and fuzzy, wearing a flea collar but no ID, and none of the salespeople know anything about him. I can't bear to leave him where I found him, so I take him into the car with me, stroking his little head the whole way home.

"*Mas prieto que mi alma,*" Ana pronounces him. *Darker than my soul.*

"I'll take him to the SPCA," I promise. She gives me a skeptical look.

"OK, I'll find a home for him. We already have four cats; we don't need five."

"We could call him Bola," Ana muses. "He looks just like a little furry ball."

"We're not keeping him," I insist.

Of course we keep him. He's affectionate, a lap cat; he purrs constantly. He gets along great with the other kittens, wrestles hard with Cielito, curls up with Mota for naps; how can we give him up? And what's the difference, really, between four cats and five?

We get a call from Kyra, our support group leader. Gene's in the hospital, in San Francisco; there are "complications." We mean to call, but somehow we don't. Last time we saw him he didn't look bad. That was when he was telling us about getting on the short list at UC Davis, but he's still months away from a transplant, we think—at best, months away.

The day before Thanksgiving, Kyra calls back. Gene got his transplant; he's in the ICU. There was a lot of bleeding, but that's normal, she assures us: she's had her new liver for four years now; she knows about these things.

We call him on Thanksgiving Day, but the nurse on charge won't let us talk to him. Then we call Rafael, a Puerto Rican friend of Ana's who's had AIDS for years; he's at San Francisco General now with a brain tumor, we've heard. His nurse won't let us talk to him either. "She said he's 'out-of-it,'" Ana shrugs. We gaze into our fire, crack walnuts, eat pumpkin muffins. The cats and dogs sprawl all around the room in their post-turkey stupors. We pack the refrigerator full of our leftover feast.

So the next day we visit both of them. It seems fitting, on this holiday dedicated to giving thanks, especially now that we feel temporarily removed from suffering ourselves.

Rafael's room is so dark we can hardly tell it's him; walking down the ward we'd glimpsed a fiery sunset over Twin Peaks, but here the window is on the other side of the room, cordoned off by dark drapes. "*Señora?*" Ana inquires of the standing dark shape she can see. It's Rafael's mother; she and Ana know each other from the old days, ten years ago maybe, when Rafael and his lover Mike, and Ana's friend Jose and her brother Adrian (now dead) used to roam the city with Ana. Once the five of them walked all the way from Fisherman's Wharf home to the Mission carrying a table Ana had bought.

"*Ay, tanto tiempo, como está?*" "*Muy Bien, Gracias a Dios, y usted?*" The two women exchange greetings, while the paper-thin man in the bed lies very still.

He's very weak, but he does know who we are. The last time we saw him was in Ana's hospital room a few weeks after the transplant; he'd come with José, brought her a long-stemmed bird of paradise tied with an orange ribbon. He looked well then, pale but reasonably sturdy, his laughter and quick wit intact. Now his mind has slowed so much we can see the effort, the groaning churning of the wheels, as he struggles to follow our words.

Ana bends and kisses him once, twice, three times, offering him her lips for the same three kisses back. "*Ay, que rico,*" she says after each one. *How delicious.* "*Me han echado de menos tus besos.*"

"Really?" Rafael asks, wonderingly. "You missed my kisses?"

"*¡Ay! Sí.*" She's like a mother reassuring a small child. She kisses him again, naming each kiss: one for *pasteles*, another for *alcapurria*, a third one for *mofongo*, those rich strong-flavored island foods they both miss.

Rafael's mother tells us everything Rafael ate yesterday, Thanksgiving Day. A couple of pieces of turkey, sliced very small, a whole portion of sweet potato with marshmallow. He even, she adds proudly, ate most of the fruit cup they'd brought him for dessert. As long as he eats, she says, he'll be all right. Ana gives her a look and she wavers a tiny bit. "*Si Dios quiere,*" she amends softly. *If God wishes.*

Rafael's sister pours him carrot juice, perches on the bed like a kid, stroking the big teddy bear someone brought. Mike comes in big and blustery, loud and robust and clumsy. This is the second lover he'll lose to AIDS; he's determined to do it right this time. "Who am I?" he asks Rafael. "Do you love me? Who's that lady over there?" he points to Ana. "Who gave you this teddy bear?" Testing, testing. And Rafael struggles to answer, to keep up, to do what Mike wants. "Tell him I'm Maria Felix," Ana intervenes, naming a famous Mexican actress, and Rafael does; we all laugh, the joke's on Mike now.

But there is little to say in this curtained-off room. The others make small talk; we report to them about Ana's health, our house, the animals. Rafael's sister goes on and on about a certain beach in Puerto Rico, one Ana doesn't know; we'll have to go there next time, we agree. The man in the bed lies very still. Only once he raises his head, begins to try to form a sentence; he seems agitated. "There's not enough—not enough . . . " "Not enough *what*, Rafael?" I ask, trying to follow, to soothe. He looks frightened, helpless. He looks at all of us, five big grown-ups surrounding his bed; some of us are standing, there are only two chairs in the room. "Not enough—not enough . . . " He can't finish the phrase, he falls back onto his pillow, defeated. But Ana understands. "Not enough chairs, Rafael? Are you concerned because we're not all sitting down?" He nods vigorously, delighted, relieved. These, then, are his last concerns: to see that his guests are comfortable, to do what he can to please us. And I had thought he was trying to make some larger statement, to tell us something about his life. *Not enough, not enough.* He closes his eyes, drifts with his teddy bear in the dark bed.

From there we drive up the hill to UCSF to see Gene. Dorey opens the door, looking rumpled but surprisingly well, I think, in a wine-colored velour sweat suit. Gene lies in bed behind her, thin and weak, but alert, pleased to see us. Although it's dark outside, the room feels light; it's airy, private, and Dorey has set up a little altar on the windowsill: a small collection of sacred objects, clay figures, a flute. "Every hour on the hour, throughout Gene's surgery, I read poetry and prayed," she tells us proudly. "I kept falling asleep, but I had a friend wake me. Before he went into the O.R., Gene and I read some poems together, too. We did a ceremony, saying goodbye to his old liver, welcoming the new one."

"Do you want to see my stitches?" Gene asks. It doesn't seem like an invitation we're meant to decline. Slowly, painfully, he pulls up the blue hospital gown, lowers the bedcovers with his other hand. When I glimpse his pubic hair, I look away; then he adjusts the cover again and there it is, the Mercedes-Benz symbol the liver people all talk about, a huge, ragged, upside-down Y stretching from his chest to below his navel, filled with dozens of metal staples.

"Have you counted the stitches?" Ana asks. "I had forty-six."

"I haven't counted them. You go ahead," Gene says with effort, seeming pleased at the idea, and so we do, both of us together. "One hundred and twenty-eight," I announce finally, and Gene lets his head fall back against the pillow in relief.

Out in the hallway Dorey whispers to us, "He's been so needy, I haven't been able to leave him, not for a minute. I haven't been home in more than a week. I didn't sleep for five days."

Dorey is the kind of self-sacrificing partner I always thought I should be. "But you need to rest, to take care of yourself," Ana and I both urge.

"He needs me now. I figure I'll rest later. A few days ago I did leave just for a few hours, though; I went to see my therapist. Five minutes after I got to her office the doctors paged me, told me to come back right away." She shrugs. "I asked them if it could wait an hour. They said no, they needed to explain something to me right then."

Out here, in the fluorescent corridor light, we see how haggard she looks. Back in the room, Gene shifts in his bed and Dorey tiptoes toward him instantly, making her face a mask of cheer and calm. "It's unusual that he'd even let me stand in the doorway like this," she whispers to us. "He's been like a little kid, so scared all the time.

"It's a good thing the transplant happened here, not at UC Davis. At the end his blood wasn't clotting at all. Davis called and said they had a donor, a sixty-four-year-old woman, but we were unsure; we wanted a younger donor, and then there was some question about compatibility. So then UCSF said, 'If we can find an organ for you, you *will* stay here, won't you?'"

"They were almost fighting over him," I murmur.

"They *were* fighting over him. Then another liver came through, from a seventeen-year-old girl. We don't know anything about her, only that she died of a blow to the head. Before, I'd thought I would want to know more, but I don't. This is Gene's liver now; it's the liver I dreamed he would get. I dreamed these exact energy patterns. It's so good to see you, to talk to people who understand," she says, and her face crumples for a moment. "Gene's brother came, but you know how it is with people who haven't gone through this; they get upset, you have to spend all your time comforting *them*. They've had to open Gene back up twice already since the surgery; they keep having to change the stent they put into his bile ducts. After each surgery he's been a little worse." Dorey's eyes fill with tears.

"You need to rest," we tell her. "It'll get better. This is only the beginning. You need to rest." We hug her goodbye, smoothing the velour on her back. We leave, helpless, stunned by our good fortune.

⊘

In December, Ana's foot ulcer opens up again. It's almost imperceptible at first, a hole the size of the head of a pin. When I notice it I put aloe on it, one, two, three days of aloe; it stays tiny, but looks deep. Then Ana feels a pain shooting up her ankle; scared, she rushes to the podiatrist's office on her lunch hour.

There's an infection, he confirms. It seems that when she took her orthopedic shoes in to be re-soled a few weeks before, the re-soling upset the delicate structure they'd created inside the shoe to avoid pressure on the old ulcer.

The doctor digs in deep with his knife, opening the whole thing up to see how far the infection's gone. "Stay out of work till Monday," he tells Ana, in what we realize later is a lunatic burst of optimism; it'll be more than six weeks before she's able to go back. He tells her the important thing is to clear up the infection first, so we're back to using Betadine on the ulcer, no aloe till he gives the high sign.

A week goes by, and the wound gets no smaller. The shooting pains dissipate, then start back up again. In a panic Ana calls the transplant center, where a doctor instructs her to come in the following day. Grimly, we pack expecting a hospital stay; this has happened before, years ago, before the transplant.

But the doctor who checks Ana doesn't think she needs to be hospitalized. The pulses in her ankle are good, which means there's enough circulation that the ulcer might heal on its own; nonetheless, he brings up the threat of amputation again. "We cut off a lot of feet," he says bluntly. "I recommend two months of strict bed rest; that ought to do it." Then he adds cheerfully, "If you never walked again, you'd never get another foot ulcer."

The joke falls flat.

"The last time I closed up her foot ulcer with aloe vera," I mention timidly, hating myself for this timidity.

"I've heard of aloe vera," the doctor acknowledges, adjusting his eyeglasses. That's all he says—no yea, no nea. We take this as a yea. Jubilant that Ana is not being hospitalized, that at least now there's something we can do, I tell Ana once he leaves the room, "He says two months, and he's right, it *would* be that long or longer if we just used Betadine. But with the aloe I'll bet on two weeks."

Ana checks in with her friend Connie, the receptionist. "How's the baby?" she asks. "All ready for Christmas?" We ask about Ana's old combat buddies, the people she got to know right after the transplant: Luis, Carmen, Roger. Luis and Carmen are both doing fine, Connie tells us; she has no news about Roger, who's being followed up by another transplant center now.

Then she mentions a patient we don't know, a twenty-one-year-old woman who got her kidney last year. In November her creatinine was 2.2; then she decided to stop her immunosuppressants.

"Why?" we ask, stunned.

Connie shrugs. "It's the age group. You can see it coming." Now, a month later, the woman's creatinine is 15.3.

I gasp, remembering how sick Ana was when her creatinine got up to 7 or 8. "She's not back on dialysis yet?"

"We're admitting her today," Connie says. Another shrug. "The kidney's ruined. It was from a living donor, too. Someone in her family," she adds thoughtfully.

I try to imagine what this woman and her family are feeling. Just then, Helena sweeps by the reception desk without acknowledging us—Helena the post-transplant coordinator with her elegant clothes, perfectly styled hair, icy demeanor. I can't help wondering whether Helena's twenty-minute pre-discharge session was the only counseling this patient ever got.

We're still talking about her as I wheel Ana into the talking elevator. "Fourth floor, fourth floor," it chirps brightly at us. "Going down."

"I know you need to take your medication, but I never really thought about what would happen, and how quickly, if you stopped," I say, stooping to kiss Ana's hair.

Ana nods somberly, clutching the new red pillbox Connie gave her. She'd acted like a kid with a new toy when she saw it. "That's my favorite color!" she'd told Connie proudly. And I remember the first time she saw the size of the pillbox she'd be filling and emptying every week, the first time we rented her a wheelchair—how these things have become *her* instead of *not-her* now, familiar accessories instead of frightening intrusions. The thought stays with me as we cruise down the highway and she puts on an Andres Jimenez CD. It's Puerto Rican folk-country, traditional *jibaro* music from her island's mountain people, and hearing it I feel almost as if we're on the hilly highway where I first heard these songs, the road from San Juan down to the ocean at Ponce, winding through lush green tropical mountains. The music is sad and bright and gay, haunting and lively at once, and as I listen an image comes to me. It's a balance beam, a narrow wooden beam like the ones we teetered on toe-to-heel in fifth-grade gym class, and I see now that our lives after transplant are lived on a beam like that. I see how terribly confining it is at first, how impossible it is to imagine that we'd ever learn to move with any ease or comfort on that thin ledge; and how, more and more now, our bodies come to understand the balance. How, slowly, we begin to dance.

❧

And yet this time I don't see the aloe making a difference right away. I grow frantic; all the old patterns replicate themselves so quickly. Ana is depressed and passive in her wheelchair; I feel cheated, burdened, lonely. I burrow through my alternative health books, thinking I remember something about comfrey root. One night after work I brave the Christmas-shopping crowds, dash glassy-eyed through the mall looking for another natural-remedies book I'd had but given away. I don't find that one, but I find another, and yes, comfrey root and calendula are both listed under "wound healing."

I remember our downstairs neighbor saying she'd planted comfrey in the garden; I go out looking for it in the dark. I find a huge cluster of fuzzy, lance-shaped leaves that resemble the ones in the book; this must be it, I think. I pull some up, scrub at the root, chop it up fine, then tape it against Ana's foot. She's asleep already, so I do this surreptitiously, knowing she sleeps soundly enough that I can get away with it, unable to bear the thought of waiting till morning to try the new miracle cure.

In the morning, I find out that the root I'd used was borage. "It's related to comfrey," our neighbor assures me kindly; still, none of the books mention it. I start over again with the real comfrey, but both Ana and I are getting nervous now. "What if there's some dirt left on the root?" she asks. "What if it makes my infection worse?"

I think of the A-word, amputation, and know that I'm just playing around, and with terribly high stakes. I'm not an herbalist; I don't know what the hell I'm doing. But there must be something, *something* that can help. I go back to the health food store, buy comfrey tincture and calendula gel, still hoping.

Back at the transplant center the next week we see Ana's favorite doctor, Dr. Chen. She's the only woman on the transplant team, and she's always been patient with us. "The most common complication we see with our diabetic patients is loss of limbs," she confirms gently. "The body tries to heal from outside in, but that can seal the infection inside; that's what leads to amputation."

On our way home I stop at yet another health food store, where I find a small tin of herbal salve. There's no indication on the label of what it might be good for, but the very first ingredient listed is comfrey root, the second calendula, and I recognize a few of the others from my herb books, too. I snatch it up, apply it a half-hour later as Ana drops me off at work.

When I check the ulcer again that evening, I'm stunned. A new white layer of skin has formed already over the gaping pink wound. I poke at it with a Q-tip, just to assure myself that it's skin and not pus. It is.

But if the ulcer heals this quickly, will that seal the infection inside?

The next week when we return to the transplant center I'm feeling optimistic, expecting them to ooh and aah over the fantastic progress Ana's made. "They'll beg us to tell them our secret," I joke. Of course, it doesn't happen that way; the nurse says only that it looks "pretty much the same, maybe a little better," and the doctor, a different one this time, doesn't even check it, just orders more antibiotics.

But the week after that Ana returns to her podiatrist, who confirms that the ulcer is, in fact, much improved. "Another two weeks and it'll be healed," he promises. It seems to be his stock line, but this time we want to believe him. "What're you using on the dressing, Betadine?"

"No," Ana says, "a salve that has comfrey root in it."

"Ah yes, comfrey root. It's been known for decades that that regenerates skin," the doctor assures her amiably. "Maybe I should tell all my patients about it." He says it in the same jovial tone he might use to tell us, "Maybe hell will freeze over next week. Heh-heh."

Later I rage, "How can he know about aloe and comfrey, how can he see what they do, and yet not tell you about it?"

Ana just shrugs. She's used to this by now.

⤜∾⤛

Another transplant clinic visit. "The doctors take me more seriously, when you come with me," Ana says as we sit in the waiting room. "They treat me with more respect." It isn't the first time she's said this.

"Maybe they do," I shrug. "Maybe it's just because they see *someone's* with you. Maybe it's because I'm white. Maybe it's because I know some of their lingo. If they do treat you differently when I'm with you, they probably don't know it. They probably couldn't tell you why, themselves."

A tall, very thin, stoop-shouldered man stumbles in, leaning up against the front desk while he waits for the receptionist to get off the phone. His skin has a greenish-brown tint to it, not the color of a healthy-looking suntan but more of a true bronze with its patina of olive—a fine color for antique metal, I think, but a very bad color for a person. "He's waiting for a liver," I tell Ana in Spanish. Gene's skin had been that color, too.

The man gives up his struggle to stand and collapses into a nearby chair, tucking his head almost into his chest, and immediately a slight blonde social worker dressed all in black hurries over to him. He's going through some tests, we overhear; he's been NPO since midnight, no food or water by mouth, that's why he's so weak.

"Oh, but you can eat," the birdlike blonde assures him, fishing around for some sugar tablets. "I don't know who said you couldn't. You can eat." The man seizes a sugar tablet eagerly, places it into his mouth, grimaces.

Ana nods. "That shit tastes terrible." So I offer the guy an apple after the blonde leaves; he hesitates at first, then polishes it up on his pants leg and bites in with relish. It's a Fuji, juicy and crisp, organic, from the farmer's market. "What a good apple," he says.

"Are you diabetic?" Ana asks him.

"No. No, I'm not. Are you? I'm so sorry. Terrible disease," he says. "When I look around I can always find someone who's worse off than me."

"What you're going through doesn't look like much fun either," I venture.

"I'm sicker than hell." His face contorts.

"Are you waiting for a liver?"

"Being evaluated. For a liver *and* a kidney. Look, I usually avoid this conversation because, well, it's kind of depressing, but you were so nice . . ."

In Spanish Ana tells me, "He's going to die. That's why he doesn't want to talk about it any more; he wants to die."

"You know how bad you felt when your kidneys were failing, and you know what people waiting for livers go through," I remind her. "Imagine feeling that sick from both organs at the same time?"

The man nodded off as if falling asleep while we were speaking Spanish to each other, but now he glances up at Ana again. "You were on dialysis, right?" She nods. "When I was on dialysis, they used to bring this old man in on a gurney and hook him up and he'd be moaning real loud the whole time, Auuuuuurghhhh, auuuuuuuuurghhhh, it was all I could hear. He lived in some convalescent hospital, but they never brushed his teeth, never combed his hair; he was dirty, he stank. They didn't even put socks on him. His doctor, the one officially assigned to him, would come by to visit his other patients, but he never once spoke to this man. And one day the old guy died, right there on dialysis, and his doctor came rushing over with a Do Not Resuscitate order.

"And I told my doctor this story and all he said was, 'He's a fellow doctor. I'm not at liberty to comment.' They treat us like *shit*," he says, and for an instant his face comes alive with fury. "Don't let them treat *you* like shit, you hear?"

Then Ana's name gets called, and by the time we come back the man's gone; we'll never see him again. "People who've gotten transplants are like comrades who've fought a war together, and in many ways are still fighting it," says our support group's publicity brochure, and I feel how clearly this is so; the stooped man and his story stay with us for the rest of the afternoon.

Hearing other people's stories helps us place ourselves; it reminds us over and over both how terribly fortunate and unfortunate we are, depending on who we compare ourselves with. I remember Ana's first night on dialysis, when I slumped in the waiting room, wanting to read, to escape. Of course, all I found to read was a Kidney Foundation newsletter. The lead story profiled a forty-four-year-old man who'd been diabetic since age three. Both of his legs and eight of his fingers had been amputated. And there were photos of him looking active and cheerful, bowling with his prosthetic fingers, balancing on a ladder with his stumps so he could paint his own house.

Of course, the hugeness of his misfortune did not lessen Ana's suffering, or my own, on that night, or on any night since then; yet his story has stayed with me, too.

⟨≈⟩

At my office Christmas party I bring Ana over to meet Marguerite, a co-worker from another department; I don't know her well, though I see her in the lunchroom all the time. I've known for months now that Marguerite's husband Harold is on dialysis, waiting for a kidney; I figured she knew about me too, yet we've never once talked, never acknowledged each other.

Now Marguerite introduces me to Harold; he's a grizzled old elf of a man, far older than she is, I think, with large, protruding ears and a face dotted with freckles or age spots. He looks to be in his late sixties, but as he talks I realize he must be at least ten years younger. He had a transplant for sixteen years, he tells us. "And that's unusual, for a cadaver transplant," he adds conversationally. He's been back on dialysis five years now, he's got a machine at home just like Ana did, twelve hours a night. Once his number came up for an organ but he was out of town; they couldn't reach him, he missed out. Yes, his wife and son have both been tested; neither was compatible.

Then he mentions one of his nephews, who's also on dialysis, and then another. "It's genetic," he explains finally, noting our puzzled looks; something carried by the women in his family, symptomatic in the men. Their kidneys fail when they're in their thirties; all his brothers are gone already, he's watching the toll on the next generation now.

"One of my nephews, twenty-seven years old, while he was in the hospital he was giving his wife money to make the house payments, but she wasn't making 'em, see? So he got home and found a foreclosure notice on the table. His wife left him, took the kids. He asked the doctors to stop dialysis. He only lived another month," he tells us.

'Tis the season to be jolly, la la la la la. When you look around you can always find someone who's worse off than you, just as the stooped man said. We're at the California Culinary Academy; it's quite a grand bash, really, with a huge buffet, tables piled high with salads and desserts, and a long line snaking through the kitchen where sincere chef-hatted students serve up the entrees. Everyone around us is raving about the pâtés, the truffles and tarts—and in the midst of all this it's so comforting, somehow, to speak to another veteran of the war we're in, seven months down and a lifetime to go, we hope. Maybe Marguerite and I will keep talking after this, now that the link has been made, and maybe we won't; it's true that sometimes it's easier to avoid these conversations, and I know now she's been living through this for twenty-odd years already. Conversations in our lunchroom at work tend toward lighter topics; usually cat behavior problems are about as serious as it gets.

Driving home from the Christmas party Ana says to me, "Talking to that man, I get the feeling that I won't be working for too many more years."

"Why not?" I ask.

"It reminds me how fragile this existence is." The tears I hear in her voice come instantly to my eyes. "I'll never be normal. I'll never have a normal life."

"Would you rather not talk to people like that? People who remind you what we're really dealing with?"

"No." She shakes her head vehemently. "No, I want to have those conversations. I need to remember how precious this time is."

And so this is where we are now, month seven. We actually went out and bought a wheelchair this time; it seemed easier than renting and renting again. Our spirits are so much better this time; we didn't fight on the way to the wheelchair store, and Ana even got enthusiastic about decorating the chair, maybe putting a Puerto Rican flag on the back. One night we even made love in the wheelchair, me sitting on top of Ana, swarming all over her, directing her hands, her mouth. Her breasts have good days and bad days now; sometimes they're so tender she can't even soap them up in the shower, but other days they're almost like they used to be and I can linger over them, licking, squeezing, even biting a little. Sex isn't what it was but it's not dead either, and anyway it seems I've finally let go of what it *was*, of wanting it to be that way again; it's been months since I cried over that particular loss.

And Dr. Lucca has lowered Ana to 7.5 milligrams of Prednisone a day this time, down from 10, but only because she asked him to; we wonder sometimes, if she'd never asked for the meds to be reduced, would she still be taking the megadoses they started her on? Most of her excess body hair has fallen out now, the pimples on her forehead are gone, and her cheeks are less puffed-out; her body is, little by little, more her own. I wonder whether someday we'll sum up this whole year in a few casual sentences, as we've heard others do: "Oh, yes, the first year is hard." A graceful shrug. "Getting used to the medications, those high doses . . . "

The implication is that it gets easier. And in fact, it does, it has; we'd hoped she'd be off the Prednisone altogether by now, but hey, 7.5 milligrams a day, down from the 110 they started her at, that's progress. They even dropped her Cyclosporine down, from 600 to 550 mg. twice daily; every little bit helps. And the foot ulcer is terribly discouraging, and so are the doctor's attitudes, but we mustn't let that embitter us, we agree; this medical system, these transplant docs are our lifeline, after all. Ana's kidney function is good. We're still in love. It's almost a new year.

EIGHT

Rafael is dead. He died the morning of Christmas Eve, just missing the arrival of the brother who flew from Puerto Rico to see him. In the end, José tells us, Rafael's mother and Mike accepted his death; they stopped talking to him like an imbecile. They talked about his life, and theirs. They urged him to go. It was a miracle, says José. Now Rafael's spirit has been set free.

He tells us all this over forkfuls of the traditional Puerto Rican Christmas feast Ana has prepared, *arroz con gandules, pasteles, casquitos de guayaba con queso,* sweet coconut *tembleque* for dessert. The cats and dogs are lurking under the table, hoping for scraps. Occasionally the kittens try to jump right on up; we maintain the peace with our water guns cocked. It's one of those Bay Area jewels of a day, warm and springlike; there are roses still blooming in the yard, hummingbirds whirring around the feeder on the deck. After dark we drive the neighborhood streets; many houses are lit, one whole block ablaze like a holiday fantasyland. We're enchanted, dizzy with light and color and flash.

Then we drop José off at the train station and head north to Richmond, where Dorey has invited us for Christmas Night dinner.

Dorey and Gene have been through several kinds of hell in the last month. After the transplant and the three additional surgeries that followed, "Gene went nuts," Dorey tells us matter-of-factly. "He was paranoid. He was convinced the doctors were going to open him back up so they could take out his liver and give it to someone else."

Gene smiles faintly. He's still gaunt, and he sits propped up with blankets on the far end of the couch, his gaze a little vacant; he only comes to life when Ana talks to him about the medications and their side effects. It's a language he can understand.

"They had to put a 24-hour-a-day watch on him," Dorey says. "Even the doctors were freaked out. They started asking me if he had a 'psychiatric history.'" She grimaces. "He was refusing to take his meds, claimed they were trying to poison him. Now the doctors think it was probably from all the anesthesia. They lowered his Prednisone, too."

"I'm better now," says Gene. It's not clear whether he's asking a question or making a statement.

Dorey sighs. "He's better than he was."

Later, when I go into the kitchen to help her, Dorey whispers fiercely to me, "He's still paranoid. The doctors instructed me never to leave him alone. But he's healing so slowly, it'll be at least six months before he can work again. I *have* to work, I'm the only one bringing money in."

"How are you sustaining yourself?" I ask. "How are you surviving?"

"Some friends have helped out, even some former students. Other people can't deal; they stay away.

"My father was crazy," Dorey says. "My mother was an alcoholic. I spent my whole childhood taking care of them. This wasn't what I wanted for my life."

We eat dinner at a long table with an embroidered white linen tablecloth, drink non-alcoholic wine from goblets adorned with real gold leaf. (Of course, following a liver transplant, people are required to swear off alcohol for life.) "Wedding presents," Dorey tells us about the goblets, nodding toward the sideboard; and there they are in full color, Dorey and Gene as bride and groom—elegantly dressed, sun-dappled, and radiant, toasting each other on a broad green lawn.

"How long ago was that?" I ask, although I know.

"Less than three years." Dorey passes the platter of turkey, the wilted-spinach salad with tangerines. She looks after Gene with the cool efficiency of a hired aide, serves him salad, watches him with sharp, tired eyes. Then he signals that he needs to go back to the couch, and she helps him hobble there, not rough with him but not tender either. Trapped, I think, looking back at the wedding picture, then at the frail, confused man in the living room. We leave them with thanks, hugs, New Year's wishes. There seems so little to say.

Later Ana tells me that she has a different sense of what's going on with Gene. "I don't think he really wanted the transplant," she says. "He put up a good front, but he never accepted it. Remember how he kept saying he was going to heal himself? For him the transplant meant giving up. He's fighting it, even now.

"And there's something else there, too," she muses. "That liver he got, I think the girl killed herself. There's some trauma there. The shaman could help."

"Dorey and Gene know about resources like that," I say. "They're not the kind of people who would think that was crazy. But they're overwhelmed right now."

Ana sighs. "I know."

Still, we call them the next day and leave the shaman's phone number on their answering machine—just in case.

※

In early January, the day after our eight-month transplant anniversary, I get sick. The flu that felled each of my co-workers one by one all autumn has finally lodged itself in me. It hits on a Saturday, so at first I try to ignore it; Ana and I go out shopping, me pushing her in the wheelchair. Her foot ulcer is healed again—the comfrey salve did the trick. But the tissue around it is still fragile, and the podiatrist wants her off it for another week.

By mid-afternoon my throat is scratchy, I'm sneezing and sniffling, and my head is clouding over with the strange, thick, almost comforting fog of illness. I make a pot of soup for us, then sit on the couch and eat in a congested daze; finally I take myself off to bed while Ana putters around, cleaning the fish tank, brushing the dogs, watching TV. I want her to take care of me, but neither of us is used to this; I'm the designated caretaker, and besides, everything is hard for her still. She thumps awkwardly around in the big Velcro boot she wears to keep pressure off the foot ulcer. When I hear her come upstairs I can't send her right back down to bring me a cup of tea. No, it's easier for me to get it myself, even in my feverish haze; and then it's such a huge relief to get back to bed, the flannel sheets and foam mattress sinking in around me so that it feels like I'm floating.

"You could come in and keep me company," I call out feebly to Ana a few times, so she does, but only for a few minutes. She sits on the edge of the bed dangling cat toys for the kittens who've plumped themselves in around me, settling like warm stones between my limbs. I wish I didn't have to ask her to put the *alcoholado*, Puerto Rican eucalyptus-scented rubbing alcohol, on my chest; I wish she'd offer on her own.

The next morning I'm not much better, but Ana wakes up hungry, as usual. She's like the cats and dogs in the morning, all her energy set toward one goal—breakfast—and yet she's particular about it; she wants eggs and potatoes this morning, she says, but she doesn't want to cook them herself: it's too slow if she tries to do it from the wheelchair, too awkward if she's clomping around in her boot. She announces that she's taking herself out to eat, which is fine with me; I burrow deeper into the covers, feeling as if I could stay buried all day.

But Ana isn't really happy with this plan. She wants me to come with her; she starts pleading with me, wheedling, naming different places we could go.

As a compromise I offer to cook her something, not eggs and potatoes—home fries take too long—but maybe a crustless quiche with potatoes cooked into it. Ana considers, weighing her options. None of them is quite what she wants. And I picture myself getting up, getting dressed, having to go sit up straight and still in a restaurant with my running nose and heavy head, or getting up and shuffling downstairs, making a big effort to cook something that isn't even what Ana wants to eat, and I start to get mad at this image, and then I start to cry.

It's a while before Ana notices.

"It just hurts my feelings, after all these months and months I've taken care of you, and now that I'm sick you can't take care of me even for a day. All you can think about is how you're going to get your eggs and potatoes," I sniffle when she finally asks what's wrong.

"Forget it, I'll stay here. I'll just have cereal and toast," Ana says curtly, hoisting herself out of bed.

"Go out and get your stupid breakfast, do whatever you want. I just don't want to have to feel guilty when I'm sick because for once I don't want to go out with you or cook for you," I sob.

"Just forget it. I've lost my appetite."

I compromise by coming downstairs to keep her company while she limps heavily around the kitchen. There's quiet between us, but not peace. I feel too self-righteous, too attached to my own suffering and indignation. Ana buries her head in the Sunday paper. After a while I go back to bed.

⁂

"Too much heat," says the acupuncturist kindly, delicately, looming over me with her warm hands. "Without saying too much, it has to do with the kidneys."

I've come to her because I've been constipated lately, a problem I've never had before, and because the flu hit me so hard. And it must be because of the flu, because of how vulnerable it's made me feel, that her words make tears well up inside my eyes. "You mean—because of having given up the kidney?"

Matú chooses her words carefully. "There's an imbalance there. That's to be expected, right?"

Outside it's raining hard, long spears of rain cascading from the pallid sky. I've come in wrapped in my raincoat, dripping and shaking like a dog, but here in this small room, just big enough for the massage table I lie on, with thin needles angled out from my feet, shins, arms, and ears, it is dry, utterly quiet. I close my eyes.

This is what I had most feared: that my own health would be damaged in some way. "Too much heat," Matú says, a diagnosis that, of course, would make no sense to the transplant center doctors. "That's why you're constipated even though you drink a lot of water; the heat just turns the water to steam in your insides. "We can work with it," she assures me.

People can live fine with just one kidney, the doctors assured me before the transplant; and indeed I *am* fine. It's just a tune-up I need, says Matú; it's only an imbalance. To be expected, right?

But what I hear is that I am no longer whole.

꩜

A few days later I'm on the phone with my father, asking him medical questions, as usual. "What's this 'post-surgical psychosis' thing?" I ask, thinking of Gene. "Have you seen it? What causes it?"

"Sure, I've seen it. It's not uncommon. The brain reacts to the anesthesia or the pain medication; it's probably like a tiny stroke. Usually resolves on its own within a few weeks.

"You're so interested in medicine," my father remarks for probably the ten-thousandth time, "You should go to medical school."

And I laugh, brushing him off as usual. "Do we really need another doctor in the family, Dad?"

Later that night, though, his words come back to me. I've never really thought about becoming a doctor, not since junior high when I tuned out my science classes and turned toward literature instead; science didn't mean anything to me then, it seemed irrelevant, disconnected from my life. In the past ten years, of course, all that has changed; I've grown so intimately connected to the body's functions, Jean-Paul's T-cell counts, Ana's creatinine—far more connected to these phenomena, in fact, than to literature. And it's true that I'm more compelled these days by medical journals than by novels or poems. It's 1:00 A.M., then 2:00, and I can't sleep, my mind turning over and over this idea. I could go to medical school, could become a doctor. I could become the kind of doctor we've encountered all too rarely: the kind who listens, answers questions, acts like we have a right to understand what's going on. The kind who *asks* questions, too; the kind with an open mind, who might tell a patient about aloe vera, comfrey root, acupuncture, fish oil.

I find myself falling in love with this idea.

Over the next few days I investigate all the science classes I'd have to take. Mills College, right near our house, has a post-baccalaureate pre-med program, I learn; I call them for an application, call my doctor friends for information. Ana watches from outside my whirlwind, quiet, amused, supportive.

Then one day she says casually, "You've inspired me. I may go back to school, too."

And so we enter the New Year ferocious with energy and hope and new plans.

⟡

On January 20 Ana turns forty-two. To celebrate we go to Disneyland, a place she's wanted to visit all her life. But she still has to stay off her feet, because the tissue on the healed foot ulcer remains fragile; so the first day I push her everywhere in the manual chair, and by the end of the day both of us are cranky from the strain of our roles. It's like being in a potato sack race, with neither one of us able to go anywhere without the other. The second day, wiser, we rent an electric scooter and Ana speeds around on her own. She poses with all her larger-than-life buddies: Mickey Mouse kisses her cheek; Goofy sits on her lap. I snap a photo of her with Donald Duck, and Mickey acts jealous, stamping his big red plastic feet. Ana laughs, soaking it all up like a five year old. "I had Donald Duck and Mickey Mouse fighting over me," she'll tell everyone later, proudly.

The week after we get back Ana gets out of the wheelchair for good— we think, we hope.

⟡

It's one of those strange stormy January days; mid-afternoon the sun shines gaily out from the sea of black clouds overhead. By 4:00 the rain on the streets dries up like tears; a blush of yellow light comes over everything, sweet and brief. In the cold, clear light of early evening I drive home from my writer's group meeting in the city, planning the dinner I'll cook, a cozy evening by the fire: a pesto lasagna, I settle on in my mind, with steamed vegetables and red wine.

I've been away from home all day, unusual for a Saturday; Ana and I usually spend the whole weekend together, greedy for the time together, yet always I feel pulled toward the other things that are also important to me—time with friends, writing time. So today I went off to the writer's group and Ana spent the day watching videos with her friend Mari, and now, at 5:30, our reunion is delicious; I bury my lips in her *pollito*, the silky warm skin of her neck.

As the last streak of yellow light fades into indigo overhead, we go out to the backyard hot tub. It's only our second time out here since the podiatrist pronounced Ana's foot ulcer officially healed, this sweet privilege given back to us again, and I play with Ana in the warm water, letting the jets push me toward her, hugging and riding her. Eventually we settle into my favorite position, Ana in the corner with her legs stretched out, me sprawled on my back on top of her, half in, half out of the water, my head lolling on the plump cushion of her belly, her hands resting lightly on my breasts—"So you won't fall," I tease.

We talk about the book party I might have, now that my poetry book has finally been published, and as always Ana leaps ahead in her schemes; I'm still hovering around the idea of the party, and she's already planning what to cook. She has a recipe somewhere for rice primavera, she says; she'll make it in the rice cooker, it's less greasy that way.

Then we're back onto the subject of school. She called last week and ordered the catalog, she says. She's nervous about writing papers in English, but I reassure her; I'll help her, and besides, her ideas and experience, her grasp of the material are so much more important than the grammar. Maybe we'll get another computer, a cheap one, for her to work on, we decide. We don't need another printer; she can use mine.

By the time we get back upstairs, warm and limp from our soak, the kitchen is rich with the smell of lasagna. Chopping the broccoli to steam, feeling contented and generous, I remind Ana, "Remember that woman who came to the last support group meeting, the one who's still on peritoneal dialysis? You said you were going to call her, see how she's doing."

It's a call Ana's talked about making for weeks, but hasn't quite gotten to. It was so painful talking to June, hearing her despair: the waiting, the weakness, the relentless itching of her skin. Uremic pruritis, the doctors call it; it comes from inside, no cream or lotion will soothe it. But now, filled with the same well-being I feel, Ana picks up the phone, and I hear her leaving a message on June's machine.

"I've been wondering how Gene and Dorey are, too," I say, and obediently Ana dials their number too. "It's busy," she reports. And then, because she's in the mood, because we'd written his phone number on our support group list—he'd said he'd try to come to a meeting, though he hasn't made it yet—Ana calls Roger, her liver transplant friend from the hospital. It's been a few months since she's talked to him, maybe more; things had sounded a little rocky: he'd developed diabetes from the Prednisone, he had a fever, he was back in the hospital for a few days. Still we've thought of him often; he was one of the three musketeers, after all, patrolling the hospital corridors with Luis and Ana in those first weeks after the transplant.

"Roger?" repeats the woman who answers the phone at his number, as if she hasn't heard correctly. "*Roger?* Who is this? What do you want?"

Ana explains, and the woman's voice softens. "How are *you?*" she keeps asking. "How are *you?*" I know this because I hear Ana saying over and over, "I'm fine, really. I'm doing fine."

"Roger passed away," Ana tells me when she hangs up the phone. "His first liver didn't work out. He went back for a second transplant in December. He died a week later."

We sit together in the dark living room, stunned. I can still see Roger so clearly, strolling the hospital hallways in that absurd little institutional gown. I remember the day of Ana's first OKT3 treatment, when I was so shaky and he was the first person I saw. "It's not that bad," he told me then. "She's gonna be fine."

The broccoli is past done already; its bright-green stalks are turning dull. We've lost our appetites. We sit, remembering.

"That balloon I gave him, the first time I left the hospital," Ana says. "Remember how he gave it back to me when I went in the second time, when *he* left?"

"He was always so patient. Remember how Luis was climbing the walls, wanting to go home, and Roger just said, 'We've got the rest of our lives to live'?" I say. "He wasn't even that sick yet when he got his transplant. I wonder if . . ."

But of course there's no point in wondering.

Ana calls Luis then; I help her dial his number in the dim light. A little girl answers, passes the phone to her mother. "Is Luis there? Is he all right?" Ana asks. Later she tells me her heart stopped for a moment, when the woman hesitated before answering her.

But Luis is fine; his creatinine is low, stable. He's still on a higher dose of Prednisone than Ana, but his Cyclosporine is lower; they go through all these details like high school girls trading makeup tips. Finally I hear Ana say, "Do you remember Roger? M'ijo, are you sitting down?"

Luis had talked to Roger on Thanksgiving, he says. They'd talked about Ana, too, but they'd both lost her number. Luis says too that all through December he'd felt like crying. At the time, he didn't know why. Now he does.

When we finally sit down to dinner I light one candle for Ana's life, another in Roger's memory. We eat mostly in silence, still remembering.

"How does it make you feel? About yourself?" I ask Ana finally.

"I know it's not rational. I know livers are different from kidneys. I know I'm doing fine. But it makes me feel like I'm next," Ana says, turning her head away.

Later, in bed, she tells me, "Luis said sometimes he 'forgets' to take his medication. I told him, 'M'ijo, you can't do that!' For me taking my medication is just like eating, brushing my teeth, taking a shower. It's just what I *do*."

"There was always something, a resentment maybe, in Luis," I remember. "He'd been through so many surgeries already, before the transplant."

Ana nods.

"And I don't think his relationship with his wife is that close. She never came to see him while we were there. And Roger was kind of weird about his wife, too," I add. "Remember how he didn't like her to visit for long? And he wasn't in a hurry to go home. He always said, 'We have the rest of our lives,' but maybe there was something else going on. The will to live isn't just what you see on the surface."

I know what I'm doing; I'm distancing. I'm trying to come up with some way in which Roger and Ana are completely different, Luis and Ana are completely different. I'm working hard on creating a "them" and an "us," as if this neat trick will keep Ana out of danger. Yet maybe there's some truth in this, too. It's so complicated, how any single person endures, how life is so incredibly tenacious, so astonishingly fragile at once.

⬲

Ana is back at work, she's vibrant again, she's making plans for school. But still her face puffs swollen with fatigue at night; still she lies in bed grimacing from one pain or another, unexplained sharp muscle aches, edema so bad her ankles ache and burn from the bloat.

One night she dreams she's at a party; for some reason she has no shirt on, and the brother of the hostess makes a beeline to her. "You're disgusting," he tells her, his face contorting with revulsion.

"I had a kidney transplant," she tells him proudly.

"That's disgusting. You're so fat. I'd rather die."

And she defends herself. "I'm sorry if you don't like it, but this is *my* body, mine! And I love my life!"

It's almost nine months we've lived with this transplant, almost as long as a baby lives in a womb.

I send off my application to the pre-med program.

⬥

We celebrate our nine-month transplant anniversary with a leisurely brunch on the deck; it's mid-February, and the Bay Area is dishing up summer for us again. The trees in the backyard are still bare, but out front the flowering plums are covered with hundreds of tiny pink blossoms.

Then we drive to the Alameda shoreline, walk slowly hand-in-hand along the paved path by the beach. Ana's energy is all right today, but her hips hurt more with each step; it's like they're on fire, she says. Is it arthritis? The ache of Prednisone withdrawal? She sits, briefly, on each bench we pass, and I leave her for a few minutes to run barefoot up and down the sand. On my way back, I scoop up a handful of tiny orange shells for her. "Souvenirs," I say.

NINE

In February I turn thirty-four. For my birthday I decide to get us each an astrological reading; Ana has never had one, and the only one I've had was a gift from my father on my eighteenth birthday, now almost half my life ago. It seems like time for another.

The astrologer's office is in San Francisco's Castro district, in the upper flat of an old Victorian. Even the doormat lets us know we're in the right place, with its starry-sky-and-moon motif. As we climb the steep stairs I marvel again that Ana *can* climb these stairs now; she's barely even out of breath when we reach the landing.

We sit in the front parlor, a room filled with plants, astrology books, and small altars, and the astrologer offers us each a cup of blackberry-cherry tea. She's in her mid-forties, small and slender, with dark, straight, shoulder-length hair. The two large moles on one of her cheeks make her look a bit like a witch from a child's story book. She gets right to the point.

"There's something rare in your chart," she tells me. "In astrology, we consider rare events to be the most significant. In your case, it's a conjunction of planets that happens only once in 240 years, so it never shows up at all for most people."

This particular conjunction of the planets in my sign, she explains, began about a year and a half ago. It's still going on, in fact. It has to do with profound transformation, with death and rebirth. She looks searchingly at my face. "Does this sound familiar?" she asks.

Ana and I exchange looks. "On a literal level, the death and rebirth were my partner's," I tell the astrologer. "Nine months ago I donated a kidney to her."

"Astrology doesn't care about the literal," the astrologer explains. "This took place within your field; it was part of your life, too. This transformation was in your chart from the instant you were born."

Strangely, the theme of death and rebirth does not figure nearly as large in Ana's chart as in mine. When Ana asks specifically about her health, in fact, the astrologer appears disinterested. "Your health issues exist only to teach you flexibility," she remarks. "The kind of flexibility to make sudden stops, turns, even a complete about-face. That's what you need in your life. That's the only reason for your health problems, cosmically speaking."

I ask her about my tentative new plan to become a doctor. "You have the mind for it," she affirms. "Of course, you have the mind to do a lot of other things, too. That comes from Aquarius." She'll offer no advice. Instead, she tells me that another important transit will take place soon. She suggests I burn a black candle on March 5, at the transit's peak; she gives me one, saying they're hard to find. As I burn it, she instructs, I must say goodbye to everything that is not a part of my life-purpose. I must let go of everything extraneous; I must will it dead.

It strikes me now that astrology is a lot like life. Certain things are given to us, things that are fixed, immutable—a rare conjunction of planets in my thirty-third and thirty-fourth years. *This transformation was in your chart from the instant you were born.* And then there's all the rest: whatever we, with luck and chance and human will, accident and synergy and effort, can make of our lives.

⊂∞⊃

Ana and I have been talking about registering as domestic partners, the closest we can get to a legal marriage. Because Ana works in San Francisco, we have the option of doing it there, in City Hall. We can pay our thirty-five dollars and come away with an official-looking certificate, just like a married couple. In most cases, the value of this is wholly symbolic; there is little official recognition for domestic partner status. But for us, we realize now, there would be a real benefit. Because Ana works for the city of San Francisco, whose policies are the most liberal in the country, I could be added to her health insurance; I could even become the beneficiary of her retirement plan. And if I'm going to go back to school, the health insurance would be a terrific help.

I've never seen myself as the marrying kind. Even if I were with a man, I've said often enough, I doubt I'd have gone through that particular ritual. It's always seemed too artificial to me, too confining, and, ultimately, too unrealistic. (I speak as the daughter of a woman now on her second marriage, a man on his third.) Most of all, I don't identify with the hoopla of marriage, the pomp and ceremony; it seems to me to have nothing to do with—in fact, to be antithetical to—the way a commitment between two people is actually made. For me, anyway, this commitment to Ana has evolved through a long, circuitous, often surprising process, riddled with loops and switchbacks, overwhelmingly personal.

So as we talk about making our domestic partnership official, I nibble on Ana's neck, unwilling to take the whole thing too seriously. In Spanish, the word for domestic, *doméstica*, is just one syllable away from *domesticada*, tame. I don't want us to become tame partners, I say; I prefer the idea of *parejas salvajes*, wild partners. Domestic partnership isn't marriage, of course, and yet, symbolically, it is. Somehow, I'm surprised to find that I don't mind the idea.

All we have to do is set the date.

❧

One afternoon when I get home Ana's sitting awkwardly propped-up in bed, instead of in her usual spot in the recliner by the TV. "I've got good news and bad news," she announces. "Which do you want first?"

"The bad."

"The swelling in my ankles isn't water retention."

I hold my breath. I've suspected this all along.

"The podiatrist said it's tiny fractures in my ankles. My joints are giving way; it's from the diabetes, he's seen it before. He gave me a note to take back to work; he wants me on 'light duty,' no more walking back and forth to the courtroom. He's going to make me two walking casts, to help the ankles heal. After that they'll make braces to attach to my orthopedic shoes."

"So long-term, you'll still be able to walk? As long as you use the casts or the braces?"

She nods.

"Well, that's not that bad, then." I'd been worried that the swelling meant something even more serious. I knew swollen ankles could be one sign of heart failure.

"There's some name for it, some French name," Ana tells me. She'd been too upset to write down the diagnosis.

"I can call him tomorrow and get it. I'll look it up at work."

"It's just that I'm so *tired*," Ana says, her face crumpling, and I bend to hold her, kissing her hair, her eyebrows, her cheeks. "I know," I tell her. "I know."

Her ankles are huge, the heels swollen so oddly they look deformed. For weeks she's been taking diuretics, wondering why they weren't helping.

"The *good* news is, I bought a computer!" Ana pulls herself upright, hobbles into the den to show me the huge box. She's bought one, all right; top-of-the-line everything, from what I can see.

"Where'd you get it?"

She names one of the big chain electronics stores. "I went to other places first," she says, defensively. "I even went to the used computer store. They didn't have what I wanted."

"How much?"

"Don't ask."

But I can't let it go. We've talked about computers quite a bit lately; when Ana gets an idea in her head she's like a dog, obsessed—like her own dog, Onyx, who lives to play fetch: if you throw his tennis ball somewhere he can't reach, he'll circle around that spot, crying, for hours. He'll run right to that spot the next day. He doesn't forget. Ana has that same quality; she wants what she wants so fiercely, so completely. And I struggle with this part of her, impractical, almost obsessive at times; I know it's part of how she loves the world, with such huge appetites, such greed for life itself.

When Ana first began talking about going back to school she'd agreed with me; she needed only a simple, low-end computer, since she'd just be using it as a word processor. A cheap used one would be fine. Then she started talking to her co-workers and came home spouting computerese: processors, megabytes, RAM . . .

"Do you even know what those things *mean?*" I knew she didn't; I had no idea what they meant, myself, and I had a lot more computer experience than she did.

She shrugged defensively. "Well, I don't want to buy something that's going to be out-of-date right away, you know."

"Ana, if all you need is a Volkswagen, if all you can afford if a Volkswagen, why are you talking about getting a Rolls-Royce?"

Then for a few days she swung back toward my position. "I don't want to spend over a thousand dollars," she said decisively. "That way I can pay for it with my income tax refund. I don't want to get into any more monthly payments. I can always add on to it later."

But I know her too well to be surprised, now, by this purchase. "How much?" I ask again. I've seen her poring over the advertisements. "Twenty-five hundred?"

"Around there," she says evasively.

"More?" It must be more, if she's still not saying.

"Around there. With the extended warranty and everything."

"Would you have bought this today if you hadn't gotten the news about your ankles?" I confront her.

"I was going to go to the store anyway," she says.

There's not much I can say. Ana makes more money than I do, yet she owes me close to a thousand dollars; she's been coming up short on her half of the bills for months now. My anger burns.

"And the money you owe me?" I ask.

She's prepared for this one. "I can write you a check right now." I don't ask her how.

Over dinner we talk about all we're grateful for. We talk about her health and mine, about everything she, we, can still do. A storm rages outsides; rain slashes at our windows. Depressed, the dogs huddle in their beds in the corner of the kitchen. The cats, oblivious, leap onto our laps, purring and milking us with their paws. We talk about our home, how lucky we are to have shelter.

But later, as we sit in bed together reading, I erupt again. "Do you remember how you said you wanted to stop making impulse purchases?" I remind her. "You know how I feel about your stamp collection?" It's remained a touchy issue between us. "Well, I'm going to feel the same way about this computer. I don't want to help you set it up, I don't want to use it, I don't want to know anything about it."

Ana's been quietly reading her new computer manual. Now she stomps out of bed. "Well, if you're going to make this such an issue between us, I might as well return it. I'll just pack it up right now."

"Don't return it for *me*. If you want it, you keep it. If you decide you don't want it, don't say you're returning it because of me."

She doesn't answer. She's furiously packing the components back into their boxes, taping the boxes up. She pushes the first one to the top of the stairs, preparing to take it down.

"You can't do that, not with your ankles this way," I tell her coldly. "I'll take them down for you. *If* that's what you want."

"*If* you want to help me," she agrees, equally icily.

So I carry the two boxes down to the garage, wedge them into her trunk. Outside the rain has turned to hail; it clatters fiercely down.

By Friday night Ana's ankles are so bad she spends the evening in bed. I try rubbing in some comfrey tincture, some Ayurvedic joint-ease oil, but neither one helps. She shifts uncomfortably, moving her feet back and forth as if there were flies on them. I make some baked potatoes and matzo ball soup, bring them up to her on a tray. I've come home full of energy; it's one of those rare nights when I wish I belonged to a gym. Instead I put flamenco music on in the living room and dance by myself; I lay the fat unabridged dictionary on the floor and jump on and off it, trying to approximate step aerobics. The dogs watch me, puzzled and curious. Finally I get hot and sweaty enough to grab their leashes, take them for a run around the block through the chill night air. They trot along, one on each side of me, straining joyfully toward each smell, each sound. As for me, I revel in the hugeness of the black sky, the way the far-off city lights flicker and burn.

I've looked up Ana's new diagnosis at work. "Charcot's Joint," it's called. Diabetes, and the neuropathy it engenders, is the most common cause. "Impairment of pain sensation deprives the affected joint of the normal protective reactions when exposed to forces of weight bearing and motion," I read. "Although pain is generally present, discomfort tends to be disproportionately mild relative to . . . the severe degree of destruction and disorganization of affected joints." The only treatment listed is, as Ana's doctor said, "restriction of weight-bearing activities with crutches, splints and braces." The final sentence reads cheerily, "Depending on the anatomic pattern and extent of involvement, the application of prosthetic devices after amputation may improve function."

On Saturday morning we're both depressed. I'm tired of Ana needing a big breakfast in the morning; I wish we could just get up and get on out of the house, skip the slow, drawn-out weekend-morning ritual for a change. I wish she'd cook her own breakfast, at least, and I could just go off and do something else until she's ready to go out on our Saturday errand run. But I don't want her on her feet. So I cook for her.

After I've cleared the dishes I ask casually, not looking at her, "Do you think we should get the wheelchair out?"

"I was wondering the same thing," Ana agrees. Neither one of us moves.

"I don't need it," she says after a few minutes. "I won't be walking that much."

"Well, what's the point of me cooking you breakfast then, so you could stay off your feet?" I blow up suddenly, close to tears. I open the door to the deck, to the cold, wet day.

"You're right," says Ana. "I'll use the wheelchair."

"I don't want to any more than you do. But I don't want you to be in pain tonight like you were last night, either."

I go upstairs to get the chair. I'd stashed it, optimistically, in our least accessible closet—less than a month ago, when we'd thought we wouldn't be needing it any more. I bounce it heavily back down the stairs. This all feels so familiar.

After the farmer's market and the natural foods store Ana wants to go by the used computer store.

"I thought you said you went there last week and they didn't have what you wanted," I remind her.

"I lied," Ana says easily. She shrugs. "*Una mentirita blanca.*" *A little white lie.*

At the used computer store we find a computer with most of the same features as the new one Ana had bought. It's a few years older, of course, but it's also less than one-third the price. But it seems to take hours to get all of Ana's questions answered, get the computer boxed up and paid for; it's 4:00 by the time we get home, we've got a car full of groceries to put away, and I haven't yet eaten a thing. I don't even feel hungry, just grumpy. What did I expect from this day? What did I want? I'm not sure, but somehow I feel unhappy with what I got.

Later, trying to write my feelings out, I catch myself wondering what it would be like to be with someone else, someone I could go dancing with. I look down and see that I've written, "Sometimes I feel so weary of everything that life with Ana entails."

The next day is my book party. Our friends fill the house with flowers. "I'm listed in her acknowledgments; who wants to touch me?" my friend Alison says, clowning around. Ana affects a haughty tone. "Well, the book is dedicated to *me*. It'll cost you five dollars a touch." She rolls back and forth in her wheelchair, receiving guests. It occurs to me that this is an act of defiance and acceptance at once; she could just as easily have settled herself on the couch, avoided peoples' questions about the chair. But she is, after all, the same woman who wore red to her mother's funeral, wanting to honor her mother in her own way—and because she knew it would drive the others, the somber, black-clad mourners, wild.

I love her; I can't help myself. There is no part of me that wants to leave. I drape myself over the back of her wheelchair, kissing her neck, while she tells everyone about her school plans and mine. It's true what the Buddhists say, I think, that the root of all suffering is the wish for life to be other than it is. If I can hold myself right here, right in this very spot, I'll be fine.

⁓

Instead, my despair deepens.

Another Friday night, and now it's Ana's knees that are swollen and painful. I come home with take-out sushi and find her stretched out, grimacing, in the reclining chair. So we won't go downstairs to the hot tub tonight. We won't go out somewhere to hear music, as we'd planned. Ana's face has that lopsided exhausted puffiness, that look I remember so well from before the transplant. The look that tells me I'll bring dinner to her in bed again. Our talk, our time together will be muted and pale. I'll be gentle with her; I'll offer her a backrub, some comfrey tincture for her knees. I'll kiss her goodnight, then head downstairs alone to do the day's sinkful of dishes.

And something in me chafes at this, and suffers.

But of course Ana is suffering too. She is forty-two years old, and this is the body she lives in. I can get away at times; even an hour with a friend, any break in my routine, can distract me from this sharp ache of frustration and loss. For her there's no escape.

"I never expected it to be like this," she tells me. "I never intended this." I'm sitting next to her on the bed, quite still, yet she can see that inside I'm pacing like a zoo animal. "I know, I know," I soothe, but the tears drip off my cheeks onto her arm. *"No es tu culpa." It's not your fault.*

Sometimes my own health, my vivid energy feels like a burden to me now. When I'm with Ana I always have to slow myself down. I want to go out somewhere, anywhere, to drink coffee and red wine, to be surrounded by the noise of other people's chatter. I want to go someplace I've never been, to stay up talking half the night, to dance.

And even this longing feels like a betrayal.

"I'm sorry," Ana says, and even her voice is weak.

I feel so guilty when I cry with her. I should do this with friends rather than with her, I know. What she's going through is hard enough; she doesn't need my sorrow, my anger added to her own. Yet anger doesn't contain itself well, doesn't take neat aim; it spills and slides, flooding me, the room. *I want a different life.*

One thing I don't want is to make love. I haven't wanted to for several weeks, not since before the Charcot's diagnosis. Ana tried to interest me a few nights ago, but the idea of sex seemed arduous to me, mechanical. I wished she would go to sleep so I could roam the house alone in the late-night quiet, reading, writing, cooking, paying bills. There was nothing in particular I wanted to do, only to be on my own time, unfettered. I didn't feel close to her, and I didn't particularly want to.

"I miss making love with you," Ana says now.

"I do, too," I say, though for once it's actually not true; I don't miss sex itself, only the idea of my own desire. Last year, through all the months when Ana was sexually dead, I was crazy with longing for her; I helped her bathe and toweled her off, raised her arms to slip her T-shirts on or off, kneeled to kiss her large, sad breasts, and it seemed sometimes that the sicker she got, the less able she was to respond, the more brightly my passion burned.

Now I look at the woman propped up on pillows beside me, swollen and fragile, apologetic and unlovely in the haze of her exhaustion, and I wonder, *What is there here to desire?* There seems to be no spark in her, nothing to catch and hold me, to ignite us both.

It's past 11:00 when I leave Ana, latching the bedroom door shut so the kittens won't jump her in her sleep. I go out to my backyard writing shed, work aimlessly on a few poems. Parchy, our mottled, temperamental half-Siamese who's lived outside, in protest, ever since the kittens arrived, mews at me chattily. It's a clear, windless night with an edge of chill. Far down the hill I hear the late-night drag racers rumbling and shrieking wildly around corners. "After midnight, my heart grows dangerous," I write. "I could want what those drag racers want: that speed, that impossible flight."

I try to imagine breaking up with Ana, leaving her and her illness behind to forge some carefree new life. The thought seems absurd, unimaginable. I try to picture Ana continuing her life, the struggle of it, without me, and the image is unbearable to me. I don't want us to be apart; I want to be with her, but in some lighter, sweeter life. *The wish for life to be other than it is.*

Sometimes I'm jealous of Ana's last lover, a married woman who never did leave her husband, but kept Ana waiting and pining for seven years. She got the best years of Ana's life, I think, the years when Ana was still strong. Those years were stolen from me, from our life together.

This new diagnosis, the Charcot's, isn't life-threatening. It's something else we'll grow used to; we'll find a way to live with it, I know. Ana jokes about it already: "A *charco* in my ankles," she says. "Maybe next they'll find a river on my back?" *Charco* is Spanish for pond.

Why, then, has this hit me so hard? Our life together was so circumscribed already, bordered by pills and doctors' visits, limits and uncertainties. But Ana had bought an exercise bike; she wanted to get into better shape, build her endurance up, she'd said. And I'd hoped someday we could walk together—not hike, not run up and down the hills around our house the way I do with the dogs, but walk. More than just a block or two. Without Ana having to sit and rest on every bench. I'd begun, I see now, to hope entirely too much, so that this new diagnosis opened up like a landmine in the field where I'd been barefoot, wandering.

I understand now, too, why it's easy for Ana to see her body as the enemy. Here she is, making plans for her life, optimistic and excited, and her body, that traitor, throws yet another grenade in her path. She's been religious about her diabetes control for almost three years now; she pricks her callused fingertips four times each day, squeezes a bright drop of blood onto the glucose testing strip, calculates the right amount of insulin to inject into the scarred flesh of her belly. Three years of this, after twenty years of avoidance. And the body remembers—not in vengeance, but in damage that is now undoable.

"Poor Ana," Julia said when I told her the news, and I thought, *What about* me? Self-pity is my own landmine, one that closes me off not only from my friends, but also from Ana. So this meadow path doesn't lead where I'd hoped it would, where I'd wanted so much to go; so I will have to double back, my feet still bare, and find another way.

I cannot bear the thought of Ana and myself alive but not together. It has been hard enough to contemplate, as I have so many times, the idea of losing her to death. Now I feel a sudden conviction that that is the only way I will ever let her go.

Of course this is the marriage vow, the one we haven't made; yet I see now it has been made within me, without my knowing or even willing it. *Till death do us part.*

It's almost 2:00 A.M. when I slip back into the bedroom, lay my body down beside Ana's on the bed. As usual when I've stayed up this late, it takes a long time for me to fall asleep. When I do, I sleep hard, clenched fiercely into my dream. Ana and I are in Albuquerque, and I feel a powerful nostalgia; I realize with a great, unfolding surprise how deeply I love this place. But Ana has hooked up with some New Age spiritual group, and has decided to undergo the group's ritual scarring procedure. I'm horrified, and try furiously to talk her out of it, citing the cost, the risk, the suddenness of her decision, but she is resolute. She wants a huge scar carved into her, belly to chest, and she wants it—as in real life, as she always wants everything—right now. I long to storm off, to tell her I won't stay to watch this thing that seems so wrong to me, and yet I hesitate. How can I leave her to these knives, let them cut into her without me there?

The feeling of that rage and fear, that choice, stays with me as I wake. Ana is lying next to me, on her back; I burrow into her, mouth to her collarbone, my leg looped over her to hold us close. We open into morning slowly, this way, and our bodies talk without our hearing them. Gradually we flutter our eyes open, let them meet, then let them close again.

"As long as you're alive, I want to be with you," I tell her now. We're still having last night's conversation; we've been having it, wordlessly, all night.

"I feel that too," she says, her eyes watering. "But I didn't think I had the right to ask for that."

"Why not?" I ask, my cheek to her neck, and yet I know what she means; it's only because it saddens me that I pretend I don't. As long as I am healthy and she is sick, this love demands such different things from us, such different gifts. "Forever" can't mean the same thing from her lips as from mine.

And yet we use that word now, that soaring, impossible word. *Forever,* we say. *Para siempre.*

Then we come together, our bodies salty and warm, and as our skin touches I feel the old reaching-out inside me again, the flesh asking for more. I move her hands onto my breasts, arch toward her as she strokes my nipples, lightly at first, then harder. It hasn't died between us, this unfathomable magic; it had only been put to sleep, as briefly and surely by despair as by any sleeping pill.

❦

Outside, the morning is magnificent, sunny and bright after days and days of cold rain. We go out for bagels, then to the farmer's market for our shopping ritual; the winter market is smaller, the crops fewer, but everything glows bright and fresh before us. Ana maneuvers the wheelchair herself as I wheel our little red cart from stall to stall, filling it with sweet crisp apples, organic walnuts, plump leeks, and a dazzling array of tender lettuces. As we drive away from the market, the sun slants through the window onto my shoulder, my breasts; the rayon shirt I've worn touches me lightly, like a caress, and at the stoplight Ana touches me too, her fingers teasing me from forearm to wrist.

A crippled man limps in front of us, crossing the street. His legs are different lengths, but his chest is muscular; he carries himself with a jaunty pride. In the next block there's a black dog on his back in the street, rolling and squirming with spring fever, with utter delight. Ana puts on a Ricky Martin CD ("Enrique Martinez, he *used* to be called," she says), and Ricky/Enrique sings to us:

Para siempre . . . Para amarnos de aquí hasta el sol . . .

Forever . . . To love each other from here to the sun.

Life is perfect, in this moment, and we are untouchable.

❦

Two days later Ana pages me at work. She's talked with the podiatrist.

"He checked the x-rays again," she tells me, jubilant. "It isn't Charcot's. My arches have fallen, that's all. He thinks it will correct itself with time. As long as I keep using the orthopedic shoes." I can hear she's crying.

"That's wonderful," I say, almost not believing. Around me, the world changes shape once again. I hear the astrologer's voice in my head. *Flexibility*, she says to Ana, to both of us.

I realize that the date is March 5th. That night, after I put Ana to bed, I light the black candle. "I don't know what I need to let go of," I tell its bright, silent flame. "I don't know what needs to die. But *you* do. I turn it over to you."

❦

But it *is* Charcot's, or something very like it. Ana's ankles, particularly the right one, continue to swell and burn. The more she walks, the worse it gets.

Early Charcot's, says the doctor now, sending her to have a special brace made. It's a thick plastic casing that will loop under her sole, covering half her foot and leg, ankle to calf, like a hard-shelled version of the Velcro "ski boot" she wore for the foot ulcer.

While we wait weeks for the finished brace—they're custom-making it, from a plaster cast they've molded of her foot and leg—Ana is to try to stay off her feet. Again. Yet her job requires her to walk; she has to go back and forth down the long hallway from her office to the courtroom, often several times a day.

"Take the wheelchair to work," I suggest.

"No." She is resolute.

But each weeknight her ankle grows bigger, and more painful. She can hardly hobble around the house by the time she gets home. I'm back to waiting on her, but the ankle throbs almost unbearably now, even when she lies still.

"Why can't you take the wheelchair to work?" I ask again. "It's either that or *stop* working, at least till your brace is ready." I try to reason with her. I tease her, *"Más terca que una mula." More stubborn than a mule.* No response. Finally one night I break down, furious and in tears. "Why are you sacrificing yourself like this? Why? Why?"

"I *can't* take the wheelchair to work," Ana yells back, her face crumpling. "You don't understand."

There are too many doors at work, she explains; they're not set up to be opened by someone in a chair. And she finds it exhausting to push herself; her arms can't take the weight, they're fragile, too.

"Can't people help you? Open doors for you? Someone could push you to court," I suggest.

"They've got work to do!" She glares. "No one has time to push me around. That's not what they're getting paid for."

"But you do a lot of work just sitting at your desk, right? How much, maybe half your job? Why can't you just do that part? It'd be better for them than not having you at work at all."

"It doesn't work that way. If I handle the cases, I have to take them to court."

"How about an electric wheelchair, then? A scooter? Maybe we could rent one, just till the brace is done?"

"You—don't—understand," Ana spits out at me again, and it's true, I don't. "I'm supervising clients. *Criminals*. I have to tell them what to do. I have to—"

She turns her face away from me in disgust.

"Have to *what?*"

But she can't answer me, or won't. She retreats instead onto that silent, angry island of grief where I can't reach her, can only wait for her, back on the mainland, each of us utterly alone.

"You don't know what it's like to be in a wheelchair," she tells me later. "You don't know how people look at you, like you're not even human."

I *do* know, a little, but only from the other side. I know because I've looked at people in wheelchairs that way myself, not as if they weren't human, exactly, but certainly as if they were different, alien. I've felt uncomfortable around obviously disabled people, not sure whether to meet their eyes—is that friendly, or is it condescending?—or to look away.

"Does it change the way you feel about—*yourself* ?" I ask gingerly. How stupid I've been.

"Of course it does." Ana's face contorts, but she fights to keep her voice calm. "How do you think it feels to be *una coja*, a cripple?"

"Do you feel like it would change your work with clients? Your sense of authority with them?"

She nods.

So we've gotten, finally, to the heart of this. The reason why all my well-meaning, mechanistic solutions won't work. Yet Ana is still grimacing with pain.

I kiss her forehead, her wet cheeks. "But you have to do something," I say. "What will you do?"

She checks into the cost of electric wheelchairs—a couple hundred bucks a month. Her brace should be ready in two to three weeks, we've been told.

"I'll just try to walk less," she resolves. "I'll talk to my supervisor. The doctor said he wanted me on light duty, after all."

Instead, Ana's supervisor proposes getting an electric scooter for her. The city disability office owns one, it turns out, but it's already on loan to someone else. "Write up a proposal, and maybe we can get the funds to rent another one for you," the supervisor suggests.

"What does she mean, 'write up a proposal?'" Ana fumes later. "My leg could drop off in the meantime, before I'm done writing."

"It's a bureaucracy. That's how they talk. Look, I told you I'd pay for it."

"But you shouldn't have to. *They* should. It's under the Americans with Disabilities Act," Ana says. It's 6:00 P.M., and she's lying in bed with her foot up on a pillow. "They have to make it possible for me to do my job."

Of course, Ana doesn't want the scooter or the wheelchair. This is a stalling tactic for her, as much as for her supervisor. And I've already told her what I think. I've made my offer. There's nothing else I can do.

And so the brace, when it's finally done, seems to represent both disability and liberation. Ana's leg sweats heavily under the thick, heat-trapping plastic shell. It's cumbersome to put on, like fitting the lower half of her leg into armor every morning—modern-day armor, strapped on with thick Velcro bands. And after the brace comes the battle to fit her shoe on over it; she struggles grimly with the shoehorn. It's one more task added on to her already burdensome morning routine. I can be out of bed, showered and dressed in fifteen minutes; Ana has to allow herself forty-five.

But at least the brace *does* protect her ankle. I can stop nagging her to Sit down, Sit down, Sit down. She can act like an adult again, a "human being," as she puts it. She can stand and walk—short distances, at least—without paying such a terribly high price.

Years before, as her kidneys worsened, I'd urged Ana to get a disability placard for her car. The temporary blue plastic pass meant she could park in spaces reserved for the handicapped; as she grew weaker, we used those parking spaces more and more. Now her doctor fills out the forms for her to get a whole new license plate, the kind with the little wheelchair symbol in the corner.

"My disability is permanent now," she announces, fiercely screwing in the bolts on the new plate. "It's not going to go away."

"Maybe it will. Maybe there's some alternative medicine that could help," I argue weakly.

"Maybe." She shrugs. "You can look into it." We've tacitly agreed that it's my job to ask the questions, to research and explore; she's got enough to do simply coping with each new change. I remember again what the astrologer said. *Flexibility.*

When we get to the Farmer's Market on Saturday the only parking space left is a handicapped space. "I used to feel guilty, sometimes, parking in these spaces. Thinking maybe someone else needed it more than me. Not any more," Ana says as we take off our seatbelts.

We're stepping out of the car when a woman yells from a car in a nearby parking lot, "Don't you see which parking space you're in? You don't look disabled to me."

"We have handicapped plates. It's my partner who's disabled," I shout back at her. "She's got a brace on her leg. Would you like to see it? Would you like to know what it's like to live with that, twenty-four hours a day?" Suddenly, I'm gripped by an astonishing fury. I want to grind the woman's teeth into Ana's brace.

"I'm just sick of people who aren't disabled using those parking places," the woman shouts.

"Well, next time you should *ask* before you make assumptions," I yell. I'm so angry I'm trembling, but my face is covered with tears.

"Come on," Ana says quietly to me. "It's okay. Come on."

I wipe my face on my sleeve and follow Ana toward the market, but I sneak a quick glance back. The woman, still seated in the driver's seat, has twisted herself around to unload a folded metal object from the back seat. I watch as she unfolds the wheelchair, snaps its joints into place, then transfers herself directly into the chair—a practiced move that must have taken years to master.

"I didn't realize *she* was in a chair," I tell Ana. My fury dissipates to a bleak shame. I'd assumed that the woman was able-bodied; otherwise I wouldn't have yelled the way I did. "You should ask before you make assumptions," I'd shouted. The irony stays with me now, as I follow my limping lover past the bright rows of fruit.

TEN

The support group meeting is big this month. There are lots of people waiting for livers, plus a new woman, Rachael, a skinny redhead who's brought a portable oxygen tank with her; she's on the list for a double lung plus kidney. Gene is there, looking more like himself again, though still gaunt. He can drive now, go shopping, even go to the gym, he tells us.

Tony is a muscular-looking guy in his late thirties who worked in construction until Hepatitis B blew his liver out four years ago; then he ended up with a double transplant, liver and kidney. Now he spends most of his time doing informal transplant education, talking to people in the hospital, in church groups and high school classes; the fiery oratory of a preacher comes naturally to him, inflected with a southern working-class twang. "The Hep B is back," he says now, matter-of-factly. "I'm on this study drug, lamuvidine, an antiviral. So they can't find the viral DNA any more, but the virus is still in there somewhere, chippin' away at the liver. 'Nother year or two and I may need a new one. But sometimes I think, why not give some other guy a chance instead?"

Dorey's face turns red. "I would never have a transplant," she says. "I mean, if it came down to that. I support transplantation, I'll fight for people to get transplants. But having seen what Gene's gone through, what it's done to the people he loves, I wouldn't do it. I just wouldn't." She is close to tears.

The redhead, Rachael, wants to start a speaker's bureau; she wants our support group, a branch of the national Transplant Recipients International

Organization, to incorporate, so people can make tax-deductible donations directly to us. She doesn't talk about her feelings; she's too busy with her plans. "We can set up a table at street fairs," she says. "Who's willing? Let me see a show of hands."

Sarah is back in the hospital, Erich tells us. And Gene announces that he needs another surgery; his bile duct is closing, the doctors need to go in and prop it open once again.

June, the woman waiting for a kidney, isn't here tonight. Ana has left her two messages now, and she never called back. I mailed her an article I'd found about using acupuncture to relieve the uremic itch. How much more can we do?

It takes us a while to get all the way around the circle. The last one to speak is a new guy, young-looking but silver-haired, with a narrow, foxlike face and small eyes set close together. "My name is Donald, and I'm scared to death," he begins. He's just learned he has hepatitis C; his doctor told him to "get his affairs in order," and he knows nothing else, absolutely nothing. "Can my kids get this from me?" he worries. "What should I eat? How do you get on the transplant list?" His wife, a scrappy-looking strawberry-blonde, scrunches in on the floor next to him—we're a big group tonight.

The rest of the support group practically leaps on these two in their enthusiasm to help. We remind me of a huge, slobbering, well-meaning puppy. "Take milk thistle." "Here's the name and phone number of my hepatologist." "What kind of insurance do you have?" "What are your blood numbers like?" "If you have Kaiser you can get them to give you your results every week; just call this 800 number." "Here's the name and phone number of a family counselor; she's great with chronic diseases. Go to her. It'll help."

Donald swivels his head around to look at each person as they talk. "But what should I *eat?*" he asks again, still plaintive. Dorey is scribbling down a list already, whispering consultations with his wife. No animal fat, is the group consensus. Watch your protein. "Does that include Ben and Jerry's?" he asks. We all laugh. I wonder if, when they leave, they'll be glad or sorry they came.

Erich takes up half the couch now; he's grown bigger, monthly, as his wife has shrunk. "You have to let go," he urges Donald. "Don't be afraid to cry." It seems like odd advice coming from him. He relays Sarah's saga in the same jovial tone he always uses. She went in for an operation to open up her biliary tract, which had been scarred shut, but they accidentally punctured it instead, releasing bile everywhere, so it took them a long time to get all that cleaned up. Then they went in for something else, just a routine test, and punctured her bowel in the process. With fecal matter in her bloodstream, she's been on IV feeding for a month now. It's hard to know how her weight is, she's retaining so much fluid. They were giving her IV antibiotics, and when they took the catheter out, her heart stopped—so it was back to the ICU again. Erich shakes his head. "But she says she's not ready to check out yet."

"That's obvious," someone interjects.

"She's an inspiration to us all," says Kyra, our group leader.

"She'll make it," says Donald eagerly, tagging along with the group fervor.

Then someone asks Erich how *he's* doing.

"Funny thing about it, the doctors ask me that and I say, 'How is *she?*' She's up, I'm up; she's down, I'm down," Erich says dryly.

Gene and Dorey are planning a trip to Hawaii next month, to celebrate their six-month transplant anniversary. After that, Gene says, he plans to go back to the gym, to try to build his strength up. He's hoping to go back to work again.

"It's hell," Dorey says softly to Donald and his wife. "It's been hell on our relationship. Yet there are also moments of such sweetness." Her face twists again. "Such sweetness, I wouldn't trade them for anything in the world."

⟨∞⟩

My friend Jean-Paul has moved to San Francisco now. Jean-Paul had tested positive for HIV in 1987, the year we became friends, and spent the first few years after that getting ready to die. Now, nine years after that test, his T-cell count having cautiously edged its way up, Jean-Paul has become the person I always thought I'd be: the traveler, the passionate one, the one who lives many lives and loves.

I drive to his place with a big pot of velvety leek soup, hot off our stove; we eat it with French bread in his North Beach kitchen, and Jean-Paul puts Cesaria Evora on the stereo, her voice a dark, sultry blend of languages and histories. He lights five white candles in the center of the table and tilts a stick of incense from one candlestick, and we turn off the lights. Now we're in another country: the exotic longing country of these songs, our nine years of friendship, all the dead men both of us have loved.

Hearing the Portuguese I think of Damasio, a fiery handsome Brazilian who worked with Jean-Paul and me more than ten years ago. "Sometimes I look at myself in the mirror," he told me once, "and I can't believe all this will disappear." Damasio was brilliant with computers, lithe and bright with sexuality. Once, on his way out of town, Jean-Paul called me from the airport, shy and excited as a child, to tell me he and Damasio had kissed. Years later, they had a brief affair; the following year Damasio returned to Brazil to die.

My friendship with Jean-Paul has always had this glow to it, this full-moon sense of risk and possibility. All those years ago, both of us in our twenties, I was a little in love with him; before I knew he was infected with HIV, before I realized I wasn't cut out for motherhood, I thought maybe we'd have a child together someday, he and I. I remember the day I told him that; we'd walked, huddling under one umbrella, through the rain to Café Flor, where we sat on the long bench facing the street, kept dry by the little overhead ledge. I regretted my words as soon as I'd said them, as soon as I saw his face. He'd always wished he'd had a child before it was too late, he said.

Tonight Jean-Paul tells me more of his stories, taking me with him into their smoke and heat. Once, visiting Madrid, he went home with a Spanish *futbolista*, a professional soccer player; they made loud love in a big carved wooden bed while the athlete's grandmother, blessedly deaf, slept in the next room. Then there was a young French man from the country-side, sweet and inexperienced, who told Jean-Paul afterward that what he would remember most was not their sex but the way Jean-Paul had asked to be held in his arms. "You showed me that love is possible in this life," he told Jean-Paul, meaning *in this gay life.* There was the Italian, Antonio, with whom Jean-Paul did not talk but made the most passionate love, standing, dancing, in every room in the house. But Antonio was also self-ish, a flirt, and easily angered; there were scenes between them, recrimi-nations, and a night when Jean-Paul drank too much in the disco, then wept with shame and pride and lust as Antonio danced for hours with other men. "The wages of passion," I say now, and Jean-Paul nods. On the table the candles flicker. Our mugs of tea steam in our hands.

I tell Jean-Paul how different Ana looks now. I see it most clearly when I compare photos, the ones from four or five years ago to the more recent ones. Her face is puffy now, lopsided; something is missing, some integrity her flesh once had.

My favorite picture of Ana is from our first July together; I took it on the ferry from Angel Island, where we'd gone for a picnic with a group of friends. Ana is smiling straight into me, into the camera, her eyes seduc-tive and wise at once, her hair blown up in little wisps around her face, with the great gray-blue water stretched vast beyond her. That was the day she had her second angina attack, though we didn't yet know what it was. Walking the hilly path to the picnic site Ana had to stop again and again, breathing hard, with a sharp pain in her left arm. We hadn't yet begun to set limits, to make assumptions about what she couldn't do. And so, in our innocence, we still cavorted on the boat ride back; and I took that picture, where she looks so young and wild and strong.

Our lovemaking, I tell Jean-Paul now, is nothing like it was. And yet for so long there was nothing at all; now at least we've reached a point where I can say, *If it gets no better than this, it will be enough.* I tell him about the depression I went through with the Charcot's diagnosis, the cycle I dipped through one more time: the wrenching, the return to resolve. We bought dishes together this weekend, I tell him. Nearly three years we've lived together, and all this time we'd each kept our own plates; I liked mine better, and I figured she liked hers. But on Sunday, browsing in a discount store, we found a set we both liked and bought them on impulse. Later as we rinsed them she told me she hadn't gotten rid of hers because she'd been afraid, before, that our relationship wouldn't last. I tell him what I miss from my life now is not sex so much as the other ways I used to live in my body— skiing, dancing, even the long walks. I tell him how robbed I feel.

Our talk has a life of its own, and the candles burn and burn. It's 11:30 when I leave Jean-Paul's house, wander back out into the dark rain. On my way home I stop at a 24-hour grocery to pick up a few things for Ana; then I slosh the car through the streets, up the ramp leading to the Bay Bridge, gliding fast, and suddenly a ridge of water in the road rolls up against my tires. I skid. For a second I feel my eyes close. But the car is still moving, still correctly aimed. I hunch closer to the steering wheel, drive more slowly.

Halfway across the bridge, I brake rapidly: there's a field of red taillights in front of me, all the cars suddenly stopped. Then I spot a single, mangled car in the middle of the road, twisted at a diagonal, one taillight glowing whitely, its red cover lost, hanging garishly from a thin wire. There's no sign of what the car hit. It's eerie how alone it is, two lanes over from the wall, with no one visible inside. There's no ambulance or tow truck, no other damaged vehicle; just the one ruined car, the dangling white light.

Death is all around me. It has never left my side.

I remember when I first began doing AIDS work, when I first met people who had HIV and AIDS, and then when I learned Jean-Paul had HIV too, how conscious I felt, for a time, of the nearness of death. With every bridge I drove across, every balcony I stood on, protected and yet not protected by the trappings of safety, the guardrails and fences, death seemed to whisper to me: *You could fall here. You could even jump.* It wasn't that I *wanted* to jump, only that I felt how possible it was, how close.

After a while, I got used to that feeling, stopped noticing it. Like everyone, I engage in a certain amount of denial each day, just to be able to keep driving on freeways. *No guarantees.* But tonight, briefly, I remember again. Death is right here, rocketing along beside us. It always was.

❧

Ten months and four days after the transplant, Ana and I register as domestic partners. A small group of Ana's co-workers meets us at the County Clerk's office—we'll sign our papers not in San Francisco's grand old City Hall, as I'd thought, but in an unremarkable downtown office building, since City Hall is under construction yet again.

The office is sterile, but the halls are filled with marrying. A tall black woman with an accent that sounds African, or maybe East Indian, rushes past us in a red velvet gown. "Have you seen my groom?" she asks. A few minutes later she's back, with a sheepish-looking light-skinned man in tow. She flicks her white feather boa around her shoulders and throws a smile our way, and they get into line. There's a big Latino group too, an older-looking bride and groom surrounded by people who might be their children, their nieces and nephews, everyone dressed up as if for church. The woman is Mayan-looking, small and dark; she's wearing a calf-length white cotton dress with white beaded fringe—not quite a wedding dress, but close. Some of her teeth are missing, but her smile is radiant.

The Domestic Partners line is right next to the Marriage License line. There are only a couple of people in front of us, two guys who didn't dress up for the occasion; most of the gay couples are probably waiting until next week, when the new mayor has promised to conduct a big group ceremony. But the low-key approach is fine for Ana and me. She's bought us both gorgeous corsages, lavender orchids with purple tulips, and our small group of friends goes mad with their cameras: they take pictures of us lining up, pictures of us signing the certificate, even a picture of the cashier we pay our thirty-five dollars to.

A strange thing happens to me as we wait in line. I don't feel nervous, and it's not hot, but my underarms begin to sweat. The rest of my body feels cold, yet I feel the sweat soaking into the sleeves of my rayon dress, running in great droplets down my sides. My body knows something important is happening.

Afterward we go to Frutilandia, San Francisco's only Puerto Rican restaurant. We've brought a tape of love songs I made for the occasion, along with a carrot cake I baked with fructose, not sugar, so Ana could eat it. We pour champagne and sparkling cider into little plastic champagne glasses; Ana wraps one in a napkin and crushes it under her heel like a groom in a Jewish wedding. We order hors d'oeuvres, fried green *platanos* with garlic, and *batidos*, rich milkshakes made with tropical fruits, and then, once everyone has arrived, we turn the music off and Ana and I stand up.

We've each written statements to read to each other; now, as we take them from our separate bags, I'm surprised to see how long Ana's is. I knew hers would be in Spanish, but, surprisingly, mine is, too; English is my native tongue, the language I live in day-to-day, but sometimes I think I had to learn Spanish in order to really fall in love. The rich, dramatic cadences, the slight edge of unfamiliarity, free me to say things I'd be too self-conscious to give voice to otherwise.

Ana reads first, and my Mexican friend Héctor, sitting down at the end of the table with his lover, translates line by line for our friends who don't speak Spanish.

> *Es difícil poner en palabras todo lo que siento aquí en mi pecho, alma y cora-zón por ti. Pero lo que sí te puedo decir abiertamente es que si tuviera la opcion de volver a pasar por todo lo que he pasado con tal de poder conocerte, quererte, y de ser tu amante, con todo gusto lo haria sin cambiar absolutamente nada . . .*

> *It's hard to put into words what I feel in my breast, soul and heart for you. But what I can say openly is that if I were given the chance to go through everything that I've gone through all over again, I would do so, without chang-ing a single thing—so long as it meant I could know you, love you, and be your lover . . .*

I'm crying long before she finishes.

I've brought an English translation of my words to hand out to the friends who need it, so Héctor is off the hook. I read in Spanish, trying to keep my voice steady. Trying to keep my voice in my body, my *self* in my body, on this, the closest thing to a wedding day I ever expect to have.

My love, my translation begins, *I never expected to want to promise the rest of my life to anyone . . .*

And it's true. This love took me by surprise, has continued surprising me.

> *Now your life has become so much my life that my kidney is inside you, filtering your blood; my life has become so much your life that I am more comfortable speaking these words to you in your language than in my own . . .*

I've written, too, about our differences. My days of public speaking taught me the importance of humor, so I've thrown in bits to make our friends laugh:

> Years pass and I don't clean my car, while you wash yours every two weeks. We have very different ways of being in the world. And yet it is the richness of two such different souls that strengthens us to face whatever life may bring.

I close with lines from a song, Gloria Estefan's beautiful love song to a lover she left, then returned to cherish again. *"Con los años que nos queden por vivir,"* she sings, drawing out the sweet notes around the Spanish subjunctive-tense *queden*, a verb form that acknowledges uncertainty, *"Demonstraré . . . cuánto te quiero." With whatever years we may have left to live, I will show you how much I love you.*

After our dinner rich with the flavors of Ana's island, after we've opened the presents we told friends not to bring—including a beautiful cotton throw from two of Ana's co-workers, embroidered with our names and today's date—we drive off to another friend's house at the Russian River for a *lunita de miel* (literally, in Spanish, a little moon of honey).

And on Saturday, sitting on the little deck overlooking the broad green river, Ana will spot first one hawk, then another, then more and more, until finally we see the sky is filled with them, dozens of hawks, gliding round and round overhead on their wide wings.

ELEVEN

Eleven months.

Julia sends back a sheaf of poems I'd sent her, a long sequence titled "Survival," with a note that says she thinks my metaphor and voice are freer and deeper now, since the operation.

Ana goes for an interview with the graduate psychology program she's applied to; the interviewer tells her at the end that she will recommend that Ana be admitted. (I'd told her all along she was a shoo-in). I've already received word that I've been accepted into the Mills pre-med program, which I will start in the fall. Now the question is how I'll finance it. I hear about a scholarship offered by a local company for "women going into the health field." The day I call about it is one day before the last day they'll accept inquiries; it seems like serendipity. Somehow the money will work out, I think. It's just another leap of faith.

Bola, our Wal-Mart foundling kitten, has grown into a fuzzy, handsome adolescent; we calculate that he must be at least six months old, so I take him to the vet to have him neutered. I know there's some risk involved in any surgery, but this time when the vet runs through all the dangers with me I hear them differently. Did I just never listen before? Bola, terrified, trembles in my arms, and I feel tempted to make a break for the door with him.

The vet says he recommends some basic tests of kidney function before any surgery he does, "just as a precaution."

"And what if his kidney function weren't normal?" I ask.

"We might recommend against the surgery. It could worsen the condition."

Some vets do kidney transplants for cats too, I know; I once saw a cat who'd had one, up at the UC Davis veterinary clinic. A stray cat who'd hung around near the clinic served as the donor; afterward the transplanted cat's owners adopted the donor cat too. I shake my head at the thought of giving a cat immunosuppressive medication every day. Bola goes outside a lot; he loves to parade through the grass with his fluffy gray-black tail held high. I can't stop letting him go out, and I can't bear to let him make more unwanted kittens, either. There are risks in every direction. What's the alternative?

"Skip the kidney tests," I say. "Go ahead with the neutering."

I remember Kyra's motto: *This is better than the alternative.* How often, in the months since then, Ana and I have repeated that to each other, to ourselves; it's such a fitting slogan for the life we live now.

A co-worker shows me a *People Magazine* with an update on Christopher Reeve. He's still paralyzed, can't feed himself or control his bladder, but he made it to the Academy Awards; there's a picture of him there, and another of him giving a motivational speech somewhere else. The article is headlined "The Healing Power of Love"; it quotes his wife, Dana, who says, "Some people treat me like I'm some kind of ministering angel. I'm not. I'm just a woman whose husband fell off a horse, and I'm going to take care of him." The article states delicately that Christopher and Dana are "still intimate." "Well, we can, we are able to, and we do," Dana says, and I give her an inward cheer.

"Can he still use his hands?" Ana asks later, when I show her the article. "I guess not, since they said he couldn't feed himself," I muse. We're both thinking the same thing, trying to imagine just what Chris and Dana's "intimacy" might entail. But it doesn't feel like a prurient interest, or like the kind of morbid curiosity that makes people slow down on the highway to check out the car wrecks pulled off to the side. Moments later those people will speed off in their undamaged cars; but us, we're here on the shoulder too, checking out our own crash; though the nature of our wreck is different, we understand wreckage itself.

For me, the world now seems divided into two groups: people who understand about illness and people who don't. Anyone who's dealt with AIDS is in the first group, along with anyone who's had a transplant, or thought they might need one, and even people like Julia and her husband, for whom serious illness has so far been only a brief interlude in an otherwise healthy life. People with cancer, people with lasting injuries from accidents, all of us can talk to each other, at least; we share some common language. But for the others, the ones who (even knowing better) blithely assume long lives for themselves and the ones they love, I fear Ana and I are merely an oddity, a smash-up they glance at and then pass by.

One night I read my poetry at a local gay bookstore, along with other women whose work was recently published in a new anthology of lesbian love poems. Most of the other poems are light, funny, sexy; the saddest ones deal with break-ups, but even those have a self-mocking tone. I read my poems about the transplant, the new "Survival" series, and when I finish the audience is quiet. I feel, or imagine, that they are uncomfortable; this isn't the kind of love poem they came to hear. Few people speak to me after the reading; no one buys my book. *These women are no longer my people*, I think. *I have changed tribes.*

If I do become a doctor, I know it will be because of this—because the people who understand about illness have become my tribe. I remember my visit to the astrologer, the sense she gave me of how a destiny can be both fixed and changeable. Four years ago I was in Ecuador, with such a vast array of paths before me; looking back, it seems it would have been so easy to choose a different life. Yet now I cannot imagine—do not even find myself interested in imagining—any other path.

⁂

Sarah is dead. The support group sits in silence, trying to take it in.

Erich says he wants to keep coming to meetings; we're his comrade buddies, the people who've seen him through the trenches. But he might move back to Southern California. Or maybe he'll buy a bar in Crockett; he's checked it out, all three of them are for sale.

"I work in Crockett," says Donald companionably. "At least, I used to."

"Hey, you'll be his best customer," I say. He gives me a look and I remember, too late, about alcohol and liver disease. "Sparkling water!" I say quickly, mortified, trying to make amends. "We can all go there and drink sparkling water."

Erich is still on Prozac. He's still enormous, still smiling. "I went back to work," he says.

"Does it help?" someone asks.

"Nah, same old B.S."

"Have you gone to grief counseling?" a new woman intercedes. "I'm Marsha; I lost my husband on January 10, after two separate liver transplants. He was forty-two. Grief groups have helped me," she tells Erich.

"It's the little things, the things you don't expect. Like when you see their favorite food . . . "

"Or smell the person's smell," says Erich.

"Yeah. Smell is a big one. I had a panic attack in the grocery store. I've never had a panic attack before. Nobody told me this was going to happen. But it's normal," she assures him. "A grief group lets you talk to other people going through the same thing."

Erich shakes his head. "I spent ten months in the ICU waiting room," he says. "The bill came to one-and-a-half million." It'll be paid by the insurance, of course. "Her last request was to come home to die, and I couldn't do that for her." His tone is even, but I see him, suddenly, as the trapped animal he feels himself to be; he can't go backward, none of the hell he's lived through can be erased, and yet there seems to be no clear way forward, either. He's at the cliff's edge.

"Sarah was such a fighter," Ana says suddenly, speaking directly to Erich. "At times when I feel like giving up, I think of her. I think, 'Sarah would have kept on going.' That's the legacy she left, for me, for all of us."

"Amen," Tony says softly.

Donald is a changed man. "I got a new doctor, I got on this study, Interferon and ribavirin. It's a double-blind study, but I know I got the real drugs, because after I get the Interferon shot—"

Tony laughs knowingly.

"—I spend the next day on the can. But my numbers are all back to normal, my liver enzymes, everything. I think it's the drugs, but it's also all this natural stuff I'm taking, and my diet, you know. I read labels now; I won't even eat anything with artificial color in it, 'cause my liver would have to process it. I'm not working now, I can't work while I'm on all these meds, but you know what? I don't care. My life is more important," he says.

The group cheers.

Rachael, the redhead waiting for the double lung and kidney, wheezes as she speaks. She can't stay long; these days she needs a respiratory treatment every four hours. "I'm on oxygen twenty-four hours a day now, but it's a positive thing," she tells us. "I mean, I've turned it into a positive thing, an opportunity for me to educate people. I'm so conspicuous, people notice me; it gives me a chance to tell them about organ donation.

"Lung transplants aren't like liver," she admits. "With livers, the sicker you get, the higher your priority goes. But with lungs, if you get *too* sick, they can't do the transplant. Of course I worry about that," she adds softly.

There's a new couple here tonight; they look to be in their mid twenties, both of them with long hair. The woman wears a gold nose ring; the man, scowling and gray-faced, slouches in his chair. "I'm Starr, and this is Benjy," the woman tells us. Benjy admits, in his gravelly voice, that he's got a "sketchy past." Now he's got Hep B *and* C. He speaks with a thick Boston accent, an undertone of life on the streets. "That para, para— what do you call that?" he asks Starr.

"Paracentesis."

"Yeah, that. Where they drain the fluid out. They used to do that to me every month, but I wanted it more often, man. I mean, when I leave there I feel like Fred Astaire." The group laughs.

"He's down to 138 pounds; he used to weigh 180," Starr tells us.

"So I spent all these months goin' thru stuff at UCSF, just pushin' the buttons they told me to push," Benjy goes on. "This social worker, she told me I could call her if I needed to, so I didn't call her when I won no fuckin' lottery, you know? I called her when I felt, how you say it, delusional—"

"He sees colors," Starr interjects.

"And she taped my fuckin' phone calls, man, and they turned me down for the transplant! All I want to do is eat a pizza. This diet I'm on, it gets monotonous, you know? They told me after I got a liver I could eat anything I wanted, so I'm sayin', I'm ready for that fucking pizza, man! Now I'm getting evaluated down at Stanford, but they wanna follow me for six months before they put me on the list."

"They want to make sure you can stay on a leash," Tony says gently. "They gotta know that if they say 'Jump,' you'll say—"

"Yeah, I know. 'How high.' It's just hard, man, feeling so fucking *vulnerable* all the time. Not havin' control of my life, of my own *body*, you know?"

We nod. We *do* know.

Dorey and Gene aren't here tonight, but they've sent word that they're fine; Gene is starting to work again. "And he's back to bitching about it, too" Kyra, our group leader, reports. "He said, 'Other people stop working after a transplant, why can't I?'" Then the telephone on the table rings, and she leaves the room to take the call.

When she comes back she's grim.

"I have some more bad news," she begins. "June has passed away."

June: the woman who came to the group just one time, the one on peritoneal dialysis. The one who called Ana because she couldn't stand the itching. We sent her an article about acupuncture, never heard back from her. *She gave up,* I think, and looking at Ana, I see she's thinking the same thing.

But it isn't true. "She was getting a cardiac catheterization," says Kyra. Ana and I exchange glances. That's the final test Ana had before the transplant, to make sure her heart was strong enough for the surgery. Apparently, June's wasn't.

But no. "They sent her home too quickly afterward," Kyra tells us. "A few hours later, she wasn't feeling right, so she went back to the E.R. They put her in a room, but they didn't do anything, no tests, no supervision, nothing. You know how they've cut back on nursing staff," she says, naming a local hospital that has been in the news lately for exactly that. "She died that night. A massive heart attack."

It's too much for one night, I think. The small basement room we meet in seems more crowded than ever, the very atoms of its air overcharged with anger, grief and hope.

Benjy leaves early, trailing Starr by the hand. "I can't sit," he explains, "'cause my ass is too bony, and I can't stand up 'cause my ankles swell." Then Rachael leaves, pulling her little wheeled oxygen tank like a kid's toy. The rest of us stay till long past ending time, though, even Erich. We have stories to tell, and to listen to. Here in this room, we understand these stories.

⚬⚬⚬

May 11, our one-year transplant anniversary, falls on a Saturday. Ana and I had talked about going away for the weekend, or out for a fancy dinner, but neither plan feels quite right. In fact, we find ourselves lazy about making a plan at all. What can we possibly do to properly commemorate such an event?

We wake to a sunny, ordinary morning, two of the cats crowded into bed with us, the dogs already out in the yard barking at squirrels. We shower, breakfast, go to the farmer's market; we've grown so attached to this ritual now, we no longer remember how to start our Saturdays without it. We load up our cart with apricots and plums, bright scarlet beets, the first tomatoes of the season. Then, our trunk full of produce, we drive over the bridge to Ocean Beach, the long, urban stretch of shore at San Francisco's edge.

This beach extends all the way from the upscale, touristy Cliff House, at the north end, to Fort Funston at the south: a vast landscape of sun-heated sand, iceplant-lined trails between the dunes, and cliffs where hang gliders launch themselves into air. Three days after we met Ana and I walked this beach in sweatshirts and jackets, hoods up around our ears to shield us from the freezing wind. A few weeks later, on one of those gorgeous summer days San Francisco sometimes gets in February, we hiked in T-shirts up and down the carved maze of trails. A few times I skipped ahead of Ana, out onto the little promontories directly overlooking the water. She waited patiently for me; then we sat together on a bench carved with lovers' initials, nestling against each other in the sun. That was the day I first named to myself the feeling I had in Ana's presence. It was joy.

Now, just over five years later, Ana can't walk on the beach. Her heavy orthopedic shoes would sink too deeply into the sand, making her back ache, and her right leg is rigid in its brace. The trails themselves are firmer, but they're steep; her angina would bother her there. Besides, her hips still burn when she's on her feet too long.

So we park as close as we can get to the water, and sit for a while together on a bench next to the parking lot. The waves sparkle and swell and break, just as they always do—just as they did the week before the transplant, when we came here after our meeting with the study doctor at UCSF, and I imagined my lips on her forehead to be indelible.

We hold hands.

"Happy Birthday, Rinita," I say.

And then, because I have to, I leave her and run down the sand, down to where it turns tight-packed, gleaming and wet. Tiny gray-and-white sandpipers scuttle here, bewitched by their own reflections. I run as hard as I can, until my lungs hurt and the small birds scatter ahead of me like ashes; then I turn and run all the way back, flopping down, finally, on a sunny hill of sand a few feet away from Ana's bench. The sand molds perfectly beneath me, pillowing my neck, my arms and legs; it feels so warm and fine, I could lie here forever.

I look up at Ana then, and wave. She blows me back a kiss.

AFTERWORD

Three years post-transplant, Ana's kidney function remains fine, though in other ways she is largely disabled; the burning pain in her hips turned out to be necrosis, caused by—or "secondary to," as the doctors would say—the high doses of post-transplant steroids. She'll need a double hip replacement one of these days, but she's not ready to tackle that yet. She spends most of her time in a wheelchair now. Yet still, she refers to her transplant experience as "death in reverse." Her kidney failure felt like death, and, in fact, could have led to her death—and the transplant turned that around.

Sometimes I feel, ungratefully, that the process didn't travel as far in reverse as we had hoped. Like most people with chronic health problems, Ana has good days and bad days; she has some symptoms we can predict, some whose causes we can understand, and others we can't. Getting less than eight hours of sleep on any single night can wipe her out for several days to come, as can overexertion and stress. She has learned and relearned to pace herself, to be flexible—as the astrologer advised—in what she expects from each day.

She is also never completely pain-free, even in the wheelchair. The ankle with Charcot's still bothers her, despite the brace; so does the other ankle, which we fear may eventually fracture too. We think it's diabetic neuropathy that causes the shooting pains in her feet, though we're not sure what causes the backaches, or the burning friction in her knees. The continued breast tenderness might or might not be caused by the Cellsept;

the body aches she suffers from now might be from the Prednisone, or from another, as-yet-undiagnosed condition. We've acquired a vast array of liniments; sometimes one or another helps, and sometimes nothing does. Mostly Ana is stoic in her pain; when she complains it's in an off-handed way, so that I realize she hurts far more, and more often, than she lets on. Still, though she's not talking about it, I feel the ache around her sometimes like a thin veil I can't quite reach through.

And yet she is vibrant in her plans, invigorated, though exhausted, by returning to school. She is so certain about what she wants to do. She'll work with men who've abused their wives and children, help turn *them* around. Her school advisor took six years to get her Ph.D.; Ana says she'll give herself eight. "That means I'll have it by the time I'm fifty. Then I want to open my own clinic," she says, and it is beautiful to hear her say that, to hear not only that she expects, now, to survive past fifty, but that she is so definitely planning for it.

When we visit Ana's ophthalmologist for a routine checkup, he inquires casually whether she's having any trouble with all her reading for school.

"No," Ana answers him, surprised. "I mean, there's a lot of it, but I try to pace myself."

"You've been very lucky," he says then, turning his head so his gaze includes both of us. "With such major diabetic damage to the eyes, most people would be legally blind by now."

I think back to the ceramic figurine Ana keeps on her altar at home: St. Lucia, offering forth her two eyes on a plate. *She is the protector of eyesight,* Ana told me when she bought it, and I nodded, unbelieving then. When the statue broke in an earthquake, Ana bought another one. She keeps it right beside the white candle, which is always lit.

The night before Ana's first paper is due we stay up till 2:00 A.M., her at the computer and me in the recliner next to her, editing. The next morning we make love, starting out gingerly, as we mostly do these days, but rising slowly into urgency. Into the old crescendo that astounds me still, leaving me shot through with gratitude and tears.

Afterward, as I lie in Ana's arms, the wonder comes to me in a new way. When I try to speak my thought in English, I literally choke on the words, so I switch to Spanish instead. *"Es el pensar que me puedas dar este placer porque yo te di una parte de mi cuerpo,"* I manage to tell her finally. *It's the thought that you are able to give me this pleasure because I gave you a part of my body.*

Ana nods, her chin grazing my hair, and we're silent a while. My breastbone nestles comfortably against her rib, above the great river of scar. Cielito

Lindo, the black and white cat we call Ana's *novio*, her boyfriend, circles around us, purring, butting his whiskers against Ana's hands, then mine.

"*Qué piensas?*" I ask her finally.

"I'm thinking of the kidney inside me. How it used to be yours."

"But it wasn't, not really," I say, suddenly realizing. "The life force that flows through each one of us doesn't belong to us. Like the shaman said, if each organ has a soul—well, I can't be the *owner* of my organs' souls. They just reside in me."

I remember, too, something Julia had said about giving birth to her daughter Hannah. *I had this feeling*, she had said, *even when the pain became excruciating, that there was this power being forced through me, and it came from the world.*

From the beginning, this process has forced us to confront such paradoxes, such seeming contradictions. The transplant that transformed Ana's life left her dependent on high-tech, expensive, toxic medications. Each of them provides a part of what she needs to stay alive. And yet, while we know that she could not have survived without that surgery, these medications, we also know it was not medicine alone that saved her life.

And we know, as well, that a life that has been saved is not the same life afterward; Ana has been altered by this process, forced to adapt in ways she never could have fathomed—as have I.

And yet, if we had to, we would do it again.

This is better than the alternative.

"Your book isn't just about a kidney transplant. It's about faith," Julia tells me later, reading my manuscript.

"No, it's a love story," argues Alison.

"But faith *is* love," Julia points out. And this time I let her have the last word.